If Today You Hear God's Voice

Biblical Images of Prayer for Modern Men and Women

Raymond J. Gunzel

Sheed & Ward

Sheed & Ward™ is a service of National Catholic Reporter Publishing Company, Inc.

Library of Congress Cataloging-in-Publication Date

Gunzel, Raymond J.
    If today you hear God's voice : biblical images of prayer for modern men and women / Raymond J. Gunzel.
        p.   cm.
    ISBN 1-55612-465-1 (alk. paper)
    1. Spiritual life—Catholic authors.   2. Prayer.
3. Contemplation.   I. Title
BX2350.2.G86   1992   91-36885
242'.802—dc20   CIP

Published by: Sheed & Ward
                115 E. Armour Blvd. P.O. Box 419492
                Kansas City, MO 64141

To order, call: (800) 333-7373

Contents

Preface

In the United States, indeed throughout the world, it seems, there is a hunger for prayer and vital spiritual practice that goes beyond the formalities and routine available in many mainline churches.

In my experience as spiritual director, conducting classes and workshops in prayer, as well as directing retreats for many clergy, religious and laity, I hear the same lament time and time again: "There must be more to prayer and spirituality than I am receiving from my church." Countless people are experiencing a deep hunger for prayer and spiritual practice that touches their lives and remains a source of energy and courage to face the challenges of their daily lives.

There is no doubt in my mind that there is a powerful and deeply significant spiritual awakening going on around us, but not necessarily congruent with conventional mainline religions and church activity. But the movement is not necessarily separate from it either. Where the two come together there is experienced a tremendous burst of spiritual energy that reaches not only into homes, but spreads out in a gentle compassion and realistic concern for larger community issues. This, in my estimation, is the main challenge for the Church in North America: to discern and make contact with the creative surge of spiritual life going on in our midst.

We cannot always assume that our organizational values and assumptions are in line with the deeply-felt, but often unarticulated and barely-conscious needs of people. I suggest that if the Christian churches are going to stem the tide of disenchantment, the steady leakage into fundamentalism, occultism, free-floating, self-absorbed pseudo-mysticism of the New Age movements, we need to seriously look at and examine the treasures of our contemplative, mystical and prophetic tradition. This is the bold and challenging stuff that produced the outpouring of new, life-giving energy that transformed history in the past. I am convinced that this creative power, the result of the

Divine and human converging in individual lives, is what our spiritual search is all about.

This book is a small and admittedly imperfect attempt to address that issue. It is offered with what I hope is an honest assessment of its shortcomings, but inspired by a firm belief and hope in the power of the Church at her best.

I wish to acknowledge my indebtedness to Christina Spahn and Margaret Kutcher who once again came forth to volunteer their considerable talents and generosity in aiding in the preparation of the manuscript. I am grateful to Father Mike Mack, sP, editor of *Priestly People*, for permission to reprint the material from the six articles written for that newsletter.

Bethany on the Rio Grande
Albuquerque, New Mexico
April 30, 1991

Introduction

Today we are witnessing a time of momentous change influencing even the most private sectors of our lives. Many feel besieged by forces they are unable to understand or control, eroding their sense of personal security and well-being. Personal identities, roles and social functions are called into question. Personal values, parent-child relationships, belief in God, our confidence in the integrity of the Church and its leadership, are all equally the object of erosive influences and assaults from the forces of disintegration at large in our modern world. Many wonder if indeed there is anything that can give foundation and direction to our quest for meaning and purpose.

Parents no longer feel secure in the heretofore sacred and unassailable task of passing on values to their children as they struggle against an assortment of influences from outside the home. Increasing numbers no longer trust religion and a shared faith system to defend and support parental or social efforts to guide and teach, strengthen character and call to personal responsibility. For their part, church, political party, or nation do not always give a clear and steady signal, articulating sound principles of shared values. Churches, in an effort to maintain a tenuous hold on the loyalty of their congregations, seem to vie with politicians and merchants in finding ingenious, if illusory and fleeting, ways to titillate and fascinate the largest number of followers to keep the bills paid and the programs in place.

Institutional church commitments to programs, beliefs, and traditions over the years have gained momentum by unreflective and uncritical acceptance, until today these sacrosanct activities, customs and beliefs bear the ruthless and uncompromising authority of gods made in our own image, embodying questionable aspects of our cultural values. They nonetheless continue to demand our unreflective obedience with unquestioned investment in our rapidly-diminishing resources. Even as we exhaust ourselves and deplete our material resources on their behalf, we realize little if any spiritual return for the effort.

Many of our religious leaders have carved out careers, functions, and social roles affording a sense of purpose and security, of self-importance, grounded in these temple idols. Fueled by their need to perpetuate and justify their own sense of belonging and purpose, they easily move from being mediators of a living tradition to being authoritarian custodians and guardians of empty and bland religious practices and beliefs. As often as not, these unbending, archaic norms for human behavior have little if any impact on our lived experiences.

Since so much of our present religious structure is itself grounded in the shallows of self-serving roles and social functions with their political and economic interests, the church institution cannot afford to present the uncompromising challenge of the Gospel to dismantle our idols, leave all, and follow the path of simplicity and nonviolence modeled by Jesus. For by so doing, it might alienate the bill-payers, the workers, the ones who fill our churches, satisfied with the convenience food of easy grace. As the urgency of our religious quest increases in the face of mounting stress, so too does the intensity and pace of change and deterioration. Our sense of futility rises as does our sense of frustration and disenchantment with traditional religious structures which had previously been the source of hope.

If there is anything worse than no religion, it must be pseudo-religion and its easy profferings of generic grace and painless salvation. For many searchers, atheism and agnosticism are at least honest and conscious decisions. Pseudo-religion is treacherous in providing the fleeting solace of an easily-available narcotic injecting a lethal toxin of self-righteousness and the delusion of spiritual security.

These pages are written in the belief that our Judeo-Christian tradition is one in which we are called to be the cocreators of ever-deepening and expanding possibilities enfolded in creation and the evolutionary process. It is based on the belief that our living tradition joined to Sacred Scripture is our charter guiding us into a deeper understanding of what it means to be human. It summons us to create life and release new possibility from within a living network of relationships. These relationships extend from our deep heart-center to one another, to creation and ultimately to the Creator. The goal of our spiritual quest is the harmonization of relationships. In harmonious relationships is discovered the real meaning of human existence, the fullness of life in God, the ground of all existence.

Through the centuries the community called Church has cherished, meditated on, and enlarged the meaning of this living tradition and the written word. As Word and Tradition guide us through the perils of history, shedding new light and understanding on what it means to be human, so too does our understanding of the profound and inexhaustible meaning of Christ as savior enlarge. There have been errors and excesses, there have been lapses in fidelity, inexcusable stupidities have intruded themselves into the process, but the community we call Mother has carried within her the wisdom that transcends culture and time, speaking to the heart of humanity and the heart of creation.

There is a tragic and self-defeating propensity of the human heart, so hungry for predictability and dependable security, to want to deep-freeze the living tissue of our faith. Thus, in place of a personal relationship with a living, unfolding mystery informing and enlightening the mystery of one's life, we wind up with cold dogmas, creeds carved in stone, ritualized faith, and no hope. Unfortunately, as often as not, it takes times of crisis, of disorganization and confusion to motivate us to return to the source, to reexamine and renew our true living tradition that brings life.

As will be stated often in the following pages, Jesus is the Sacrament of divine self-revelation and divine self-giving; but Jesus is also the Sacrament that is the revelation of the meaning of the human person. When one encounters Jesus, the Christ of God, in an honest and open manner, one encounters the most clear and dramatic revelation of the mystery and the meaning of one's unique self. As one meets Jesus as personal savior revealing the truth of God, one likewise meets the perfect revelation of the totally unique and irrepeatable self. In meeting this revelation, one is called to let go of and leave behind everything that had previously seemed important and necessary. With Abraham and Sarah we are called to pack our bags, leave the comfort of predictable security, and walk into the unknown promise of our unfolding life.

Authentic religion is heavy stuff. There is no neutral ground, no bargains or shortcuts. It is a clear, unambiguous, and bold summons to live life adventurously, to plunge into the mystery still enshrouded in darkness, and by one's energetic engagement, find the light, bring forth truth, establish harmony. The cost of cheap grace is spiritual death preceded by a life of increasing distress and anguish of spirit, the wages for a life lived in the shallows. The price of authentic religion is high: nothing less than the cross, eucharistic service, spiritual poverty, nonviolence and simplicity, and this in the midst of a world infatuated by violence and self-absorbed pleasure-seeking. The reward is peace grounded on the unshakable and immovable bedrock of the life of God, eternal and infinite. The life of God becomes one with the believer and passes into the world and history. Divine love frees human love to be given in compassionate service. This love and service are not imposed as a decree from without, a duty to be performed to win salvation, but spring up from within as a genuine and spontaneous expression of who one knows oneself to be at the heart-center. For life to be nourished by the living waters of our tradition, there can be no conciliation or compromise. What is required is only a bold and unambiguous "Yes" to gospel values, to be a disturbing countersign in the midst of the seductive enticements of a world that has forgotten its true purpose and identity.

Because the religious dimension of our lives, properly understood, radically affirms and awakens humanity's fundamental urge to greatness, to be the author of one's life, to be the cocreator of the world, it seems not an exaggeration to suggest that enlightened religion alone holds out for us the only hope and promise of moving through these times with boldness to the new order awaiting beyond the horizon of our limited perceptions. It sets us about the task of digging into ourselves and finding again our lost, forgotten greatness, our call to be co-creators of a restored humanity. Contrary to the fond belief of many, religion does not promise a path around the crisis, but leads right into the midst of the storm. Just as Moses and the Israelites were challenged to plunge into the realm of chaos that could have annihilated them, we too are called to face into the dilemmas, the threatening catastrophes that seem about to overwhelm and annihilate us. Moses and the Israelites were challenged to plunge into the realm of the powers of chaos where they found the power of their mighty God. Accepting the invitation to forge a divine/human covenant, a new humanity was forged in the death-defying plunge into the sea, the realm of chaos.

In our lives we follow Jesus into the desert, the wilderness solitude where the power of the Evil One holds sway over the hearts of men and women, the very evil that we fear will devour us at any moment. We are challenged to look into the teeth of this evil, to repudiate its lying bluff, denounce its shallow profferings of cheap salvation, and move into a new self-understanding. Through this soul-shattering encounter, the vision of the Mount of Beatitudes emerges as our charter for a new order of humanity and creation. Moses and the Israelites could not get to the Promised Land without the purification in the desert which opened them to the revelation of God's law, lost and long-forgotten but nonetheless imprinted on the flesh of their hearts. We cannot hope to arrive at the Mountain of the Beatitudes without a courageous journey into the realm of darkness in the wilderness of our hearts. The revelation of Sinai was the revelation of the forgotten truth of the nobility and sacredness of the human person. The Beatitudes are a continuation of that same revelation, deepening and enlarging our understanding of our long-forgotten truth, waiting to be rediscovered and brought forth from the lost center of our true selves.

In the following pages, I will suggest that the Judeo-Christian heritage lives and derives its nourishment only when it rests on a firm tripod of three mutually-interacting realities. These realities in turn are connected to the deep, inner truth of unfolding and always-growing human self-awareness. Thus the Judeo-Christian religious heritage, through the millennia, through its mythical heroes and heroines, images and symbols, pierces human consciousness and awakens us to a knowledge of who we truly are at the core of our being, calling us to respond single-heartedly to our innate dignity and divinely authored purpose. Thus, obedience to God is really obedience to the imperatives of our truest self. Sin, disobedience to God, is infidelity to our own sacred truth.

An examination of our myth reveals that our tradition is essentially contemplative, mystical, and prophetic. Because these concepts have been misused and distorted in the past, it will be helpful to reestablish them within their proper context.

Contemplation, rather than being a process of disengagement from life, describes a stance of openness that allows divine wisdom, the "Word," to inform and guide one's life. A contemplative person is one who maintains an open and responsive attitude to the many-faceted aspects of the lived experience. Contemplation involves an awareness of, and trust in life as an unfolding process, divinely authored, to be lived consciously with intent and deliberation. To be contemplative is to be mindful, awake. For the Christian contemplative, Sacred Scripture, joined to our living communal experience of faith handed down through history, is the light that enlightens our understanding of our particular and shared contemporary experience. It stretches the boundaries of consciousness to reveal alternative life-giving responses to our historical circumstances. Contemplation sensitizes and penetrates the heart-center and allows the contemporary historical experience to be a part of one's own self understanding. For the Christian, there is only one way to be present to the world, that is, as a contemplative listening to the Word of God continuing to call creation and humanity into the service of divine wisdom. There is only one way to pray and worship, that is, from a contemplative heart where the cry of the earth and her children are one with our personal self-understanding and longing for the divine.

Mystical describes the quality of consciousness that has been pierced and awakened to the reality of divine wisdom, presence, and action in every dimension and quarter of creation and history. It is the normal and expected fruit of one who truly prays from the heart. Mystics are not glassy-eyed eccentrics gazing at the sky, averting their attention from earthy matters, pathetically waiting with bated breath for the next "religious experience." The genuine mystic is a realist, feet planted firmly on the ground. The mind of the mystic has been released from the narrowness of mere sense perceptions, the bondage of purely rational, analytical processes, determined and qualified by unenlightened self-interests. The mystic is one who stands flat-footed in the midst of the predicament of the person and creation, the sin with the grace, seeing the unvarnished truth without losing sight of the whole. The mystic knows from experience that the mighty God who brings order and light from chaos and darkness continues to be present in our darkest moments, our most horrible sins and failures. The mystic is not blinded by the seen, but sees through to that which is unseen. Mysticism, far from being abnormal, is the norm for human consciousness. The mystic is the one to whom we can look for sure and true guidance. They are the ones whose minds and hearts are grounded in the unshakable conviction of the innate soundness, truth and goodness of humanity and creation, oftentimes lost in the din and clamor of our daily struggles and the creative historical process. They are the scouts who have been to the inner and outer reaches of our common journey, guiding us through uncharted territory. They have been to where creation and humanity are all going. They see what all of us are capable of seeing if we would open our hearts and believe. All of us are on the mystic journey; there are no armchair travelers, no cheering sections. Each in our own way is called to be the mystic traveller who guides and supports, encourages and cajoles our brothers and sisters on our common journey to truth.

Because we are contemplative mystics standing in the world with eyes, ears, and hearts freed to be nourished on unseen, but nonetheless true reality, we participate in life with boldness and courage. We are not afraid of the unknown journey, nor are we afraid to challenge and repudiate those forces impeding progress. Thus, we are a prophetic people. The Church is a gathering of contemplative, mystic prophets.

We are not prophets in the sense so often applied to the prophetic charism. We are prophets grounded in the clear and courageous stance confronting and repudiating whatever force impedes our forward progress, whether that force be political, social or religious. Thus, the prophet disconcerts the status quo, challenges conventional assumptions and the self-appointed guardians of mediocrity who seek to keep humanity docile and tamed to their own diminished proportions. Neither pope, priest, housewife, politician, corporate executive, or local school board is safe from the disconcerting truth joined to the bold word and action of the contemplative-mystic-prophet. To be truly awake with mind, heart and body joined in harmonious interaction is what our religious tradition is really all about.

Lest the powerful charismatic gifts of contemplation, mysticism and prophetism fall into the pit of our inflated ego, individual or group, we need to remember that an authentically-functioning church, truly grounded in the living waters of our tradition, provides the nourishing affirmation along with a strong call to personal accountability necessary for a community of contemplative, mystic prophets with a corresponding powerful presence in history.

When Church, local, national or international, becomes fascinated and obsessed with its organizational and administrative trivia, becomes concerned only with the preservation and perpetuation of its own power and control, baby pablum is meted out to dull and blunt our true spiritual hunger and lull us into a docile and comfortable slumber. We are content to light our candles, pray our devotions, nod our unreflective assent to prepackaged truisms, leaving the authorship of life to others. The deep wellsprings of the heart-center are cut off from creative participation in life. Fundamental questions surrounding the meaning of one's personal suffering, the larger significance of pain and failure, dreams and hopes, and our heartfelt desire to find solutions for the mysteries of life are untouched, even unrecognized by the meager nourishment of church-sponsored convenience food. Personal confusion, alienation and chaos will reign in our spirits unrequited, unacknowledged and therefore never brought into conscious participation in the Paschal mystery. When one person, one parish community, one national community of believers reclaims their rightful charism to be the contemplative, mystic, and prophetic presence of Christ in the world, then the world, one person, one church community at a time, continues its journey towards truth.

This book is written in the hope that the reader will be challenged to reflect on her or his personal mystery in relation to the cry of God coming to us through the cry of the earth and her children at this time in our history.

"If today you hear God's voice . . ."

Chapter 1

Moses:
Model of a Contemplative,
Mystic Prophet

Prayer, we learned in catechism, is a lifting of the mind and heart to God. The lifting of the mind and heart indicates an opening of our deepest self to a God who listens to the cry of our heart. There is an expectation that we will be attended to. Our cry, we believe, is important to the God to whom we open our heart and mind.

The most fundamental image we have of prayer is one of a dramatic dialogue being acted out on the stage of human history. We begin our understanding of prayer not by theological definitions or abstract propositions. We learn from the drama of a human struggle with political, social, and religious tyranny. The encounter between Moses and the God of Israel is a paradigm of humanity's struggle to give meaning to life, to reach beyond the time-bound, earth-bound frontiers of human experience for meaning (Ex 3:4). Prayer, in our tradition, is not a mandate from without, but rather an imperative imprinted deep within our fleshed humanity. Our understanding of prayer arises from a historical dialogue between a people agonizing in their oppression and a God who self-reveals in a response of compassion and mercy that lifts the people to an unprecedented leap into freedom. From the depths of their misery and oppression they discover an inner power for self-direction, an autonomous existence under the unmediated sovereignty of their Lord in whose image they are made.

As we follow the drama, we discover the unwrapping of a two-sided revelation exposing to our view not only a new and startling image of God, but an equally astonishing new revelation of humanity. A fundamental principle of our Judeo-Christian faith emerges: Divine self-rev-

1

elation unwraps in the same process new dimensions of human reality. As God self-reveals from within the historical moment, so too is humanity led to probe deeper into a realization of what it means to be human, created in the Divine Image, endowed with godlike qualities, urging themselves forward into human consciousness and historical action. The human struggle through history is a deepening of self-understanding. As the horizons of human consciousness enlarge in the dynamic act of living, we come to know ourselves in ever new and deepening ways. As our self-understanding unfolds, so too does our understanding of the God who created us. Growing self-awareness is the channel of divine revelation; that which inhibits the free development of the person in self-knowledge likewise inhibits and distorts the unique self-revelation of God taking place in that person.

Our understanding of prayer has its roots deep within the enfleshed human struggle to bring order and life to the chaos and darkness that surround us. As we witness the unfolding drama between Moses and the God of Israel, we discover a God intimately engaged in the historical tensions and the unfolding struggles of a people who taste bitterly the failures and poverty of their human efforts to find meaning and understanding even within their darkest moments. As their bitterness flows over them, we see them discover a long-forgotten reality, a truth hidden deeply within the remote memory of the human person. That is, that the pain of their present predicament is, in itself, a reminder of their long-forgotten dignity. Their natural longing for freedom is a reminder of a lost and forgotten space in their hearts that will not allow them to rest content in their slavery.

As they cry out from the deep of their misery to their God, they, by that very cry coming from their heart, awaken to the possibility of freedom. Their suffering is transformed into energy, a fiercely-focused drive for the freedom and dignity for which they have been created and without which they will not rest.

From our privileged vantagepoint, we discover something about what our faith tradition tells us of our own relationship with God. We plumb the depths of a theology of prayer and faith, life and action in a world that oftentimes appears to be just too much to bear, too confusing and chaotic, a world and a life of which we oftentimes are tempted to despair.

Is it any wonder that throughout human history we have succumbed to movements that seek to place God, salvation, peace and happiness beyond the frontiers of this life onto a realm of otherworldly spiritual bliss and carefree beatitude? There seems to be an innate desire to split reality into pieces: to separate spirit from matter, body from soul, God, heaven, and bliss from time and earth. Our determination to tidy up reality into categories of good and bad, ugly and beautiful, sin and grace, prevents us from seeing life even in death, beauty in ugliness, hope where there is despair. We fail to see the possibility of grace in the ugliest sin, the saint in the worst sinner, and, yes, the sinner in the greatest saint. The sad result is discouragement, despair, cynicism. As we gaze at the turmoil and chaos of the world around us, we are overwhelmed by the sheer immensity of the problems of our time. It is so tempting to seek the comfort and solace of a promised time and place removed from the pain and despair of the present.

As we peer into the meaning of this most fundamental image of humanity's relationship with God, we realize we are being turned, not away from the struggle of life, but squarely into it. There we find the God who redeems, who leads to freedom, not away from but into and through the tears, the sin, the pain and the struggle of this fleshed existence. The drama of Moses and the Israelites presents to us a two-sided tapestry revealing God and humanity mutually engaged in the creative unfolding of human history. In this gutsy engagement of a reciprocal divine/human revelation, we must come to grips with the stark and uncompromising fact that in our tradition God and humanity encounter one another in the blood, sweat, dust, tears and sin of history. In the divine/human dialogue God is revealed, but so too is the lost and hidden aspect of humanity that makes us kin to the divine, our fleshed existence the sacrament of divine revelation.

We bear deep within us the divine qualities of freedom, compassion, and justice; in a word: charity. Through these qualities we most fully realize our reciprocal relationship with God. As we pursue our natural and innate desire to experience meaning, to grapple with the mystery of our life, we encounter the presence of God living in and sharing our own fleshed life. At the same time we uncover the hidden power of the truth of our own unrecognized and unrealized humanity created in the divine image, destined to live in union with God here, now. Our lives are ordained to give presence and redemptive action to God through our own godlike qualities of freedom, justice, compassion. Charity sums up the reality of humanity and divinity coming together and living as one.

In this process, Divine Compassion is revealed in redemptive action, and the drive for liberation and truth is revealed in the cry of the heart. This human struggle is the matrix from which divine revelation unfolds. As divinity self-reveals through the endless "sending" of the divine Word to redeem and call the heart of the people to God, deeper and deeper layers of the human heart are revealed as containing ever new possibilities of human potential. Human revelation and divine revelation are warp and woof of the fabric revealing the divine/human enterprise evolving in ever greater and clearer detail throughout history.

In our individual lives, the drama of the divine/human enterprise continues. Each of us fits into the tapestry. Our lives enter into and become part of the drama. Our pain, our tears become one with all the human tears, sweat, blood of people throughout history. As our hearts and minds are raised to God, so too are the tears and struggles of humankind.

Moses is the prototype person whose heart is filled with the pain of the people. The heart opened to the plight of the human struggle is the heart touched and empowered by God. Through the heart of Moses, God returned in power to the people and broke the bonds of slavery.

When the human heart seeks to narcotize the pain of the search for meaning and order, to turn from human suffering and confusion, God is denied entrance into our affairs. The heart is denied the power of grace and becomes increasingly closed in on its impoverished resources. When this happens on a social or cultural level, human affairs fall ever deeper into chaos and darkness. The situation becomes increasingly hopeless to our limited perceptions. The only solution is increased narcotizing behavior on the part of more and more persons.

The redemptive moment comes when the heart and mind are broken from their self-protective and counterproductive stance of denial and avoidance. What has previously been a demoralizing and enervating stance now becomes transformed into new energy. Like Moses and the Prophets, we allow the Divine One to have the moment. In the surrender, Divine power sweeps into the spaces of our broken hearts. New possibility is glimpsed, courage is awakened, action is forthcoming and a new humanity is born.

Moses is our prototype. He is a threshold person imaging not only the power of God, but the power of a person united to God through a total surrender of mind and heart. Our image of prayer is, before all else, of a person immersed in a realistic engagement with the historical moment involving an honest assessment of one's impoverishment and a surrender in faith to a power beyond one's self-narcotizing efforts. True prayer is dynamic, recreative empowerment plunging us deeply into our own center where we encounter the abyss of God's infinite power and ultimately into unprecedented and unpredictable prophetic action.

In each one of us a new humanity waits to be born. Each of us is a new possibility for all humanity. Prayer is the threshold through which we meet God and the true self created in the Divine Image.

Chapter 2

Mary:
Model of a Contemplative, Mystic, Prophetic Church

Prayer is not a legal or cultic mandate imposed from without, but an awakening to a personal inner imperative. Whatever Moses saw or heard, it was not unrelated to an inner event occurring deep within his soul. The experience of Moses would become a reality awakened deep within the soul of the Hebrew people. Whatever else we might say about the historical reality of these events, we are most certainly dealing with a momentous event deep within the human psyche that reverberates as much with us today as it did with those people of so long ago.

Moses knew he was in the presence of the holy; he was on a sacred spot where one must remove the sandals. For Moses the realization dawned that the holy was not remote, distant and uninvolved, but identified with the flow of history, working in and with specific persons. Abraham, Isaac, Jacob had been infused with the divine presence in power, guiding and shaping history. Now that same divine presence was communicating with and challenging Moses. Divinity and humanity were mutually engaged. The holy is not numinous, but a divine power penetrating into and becoming one with human flesh and action. It subverts the political, socioeconomic and religious regime that oppresses and enslaves the human spirit (Exodus 3).

The presence of God is known in power; God's holy Word is one with saving, healing action. This divine presence in action is mediated through human cooperation. As the person encounters this Holy One, succumbs to it, the soul is enlarged, awakened to individual responsibility. The cry of the heart is translated into focused action in response to the historical situation. Moses' heart filled with the pain of the people, became the channel through which divine compassion entered history. Moses was given a task and the power to accomplish it. This dialogue with Divine Wisdom made him realize that he, and not God alone, would have to bear the weight of action.

This is the heart and soul of Israel's faith. It is the matrix upon which is built the structure of our Judeo-Christian revelation fulfilled in the Word Incarnate. Isreal is the mystic people who envision a new possibility for humanity. Our worship, public and private, all liturgy and sacrament commemorate this abiding presence in action and power throughout our history. Prayer is the sum total of all the disciplines of sacred times and places, words and gestures designed to open our lives to the penetration of the Word. Through prayer, the sacred events of Moses and Israel continue to penetrate history. Idolatry is forgetting the end and sacralizing mechanical gestures with archaic traditions, substituting them for personal encounters with these living events. When religion with its bureaucratic structures becomes preoccupied with its existence and the perpetuation of authority, it seduces the faithful into a spiritual dependency that leaves the heart and spirit untouched.

Jesus Christ was first recognized and identified as the new Moses. The evangelists go to great length to connect Jesus to this tradition of the eternal sending of the Word in power. Luke presents Mary as the sign of the dawn of a new epoch in the evolving consciousness of the people. In the Mosaic covenant the Word was mediated through the law and Moses was God's spokesperson. In the New Covenant, humanity is led to a new and daring realization unimaginable to the mind of the people of Moses' day.

As mentioned above, Moses' encounter awakened him to a sense of personal responsibility for the historical situation. His action was a direct response to this inner/outer event. Jeremiah began to hint at a day when the Spirit would be poured into the hearts of the people (Jer.31:31-34). The people looked to a time when the earth would be cleansed and the human heart opened to receive the Messiah who would come in power to establish a reign of divine righteousness.

The story of the virgin birth, with typical biblical ingenuity and un-compromising honesty, punches through theological formulas and aca-demic abstractions to reveal a dramatic and evolutionary leap in the divine agenda. The new revelation confounds and tantalizes our im-poverished logic and trivial imaginations. The image reveals a divine self-giving that is at the same time an emptying. The epitome of divine compassion leads God to become one with us in our human condition. Again we are confronted with the other side of revelation. That God could become one with human flesh indicates that humanity is compati-ble with, and open to, union with the divine (Eph. 3:14-19).

Divine union is not an abstract, intellectual ideal, but an existential, historical reality realized in specific detail through Mary and in Jesus the Christ. In this divine intervention a new epoch opened in history. No longer is the relationship between God, the Divine Word, and hu-manity mediated through Moses and the Law. Human flesh is the Ark of the new Covenant. All human flesh, and through human flesh all creation, is united to welcome the penetration of divine life. Every human person is invited to become the temple wherein humanity and divinity are once again united in history to draw creation to its divinely appointed end. Mary becomes the prototype of the new temple, the new church realizing the Christ-event through history. Mary is also the model of the new person, impregnated with the seed of divine life, making love, compassion, and justice a reality in human action.

Into Mary's virginal womb the Word penetrates and takes on flesh. Mary's soul, like Moses', is awakened to her individual role and re-sponse to this event. The "Magnificat" is the cry of her heart awaken-ing to the frightening reality that God's promise to the people will be realized in her. The revolutionary, subversive agenda of redemptive Wisdom makes a quantum leap that will open the human consciousness to a new realization of personal responsibility and participation in bringing about the hoped-for day of the Lord.

The God of our revelation enters history with sweeping power, opens and lifts the person to a participation in that same divine power and wisdom. The price for this awakening to new horizons of human possibility is to be set against conventional wisdom concretized in the structures of culture and manifest in the political, socioeconomic, and religious institutions of society. The opening of the mind to truth sensitizes us to the reality of the reign of sin, the tyranny of oppressive stereotypes and their tenacious hold on the minds and hearts of persons. We awaken to the fact that oftentimes religion, with its rituals and symbols, its laws and traditions, does no more than reinforce and give an aura of propriety to mindless loyalties. Mary marveled and exulted that her Lord would topple the mighty from their thrones and raise up the lowly; God would fill the hungry and dismiss those who were satisfied (Lk.1:46-55).

With Mary's surrender, the Divine agenda for humanity, inaugurated by Moses and his encounter with God at the burning bush, is in place.

Throughout the centuries preceding the Incarnation of Christ, the Israelites had come to experience God as the One that could not be contained or known by name. The God of the Israelites was not predictable, easily managed and manipulated by human devices. Resisting what appears to be an innate tendency to take charge, even of the Divine One, to tuck the Almighty One into our pocket and reduce the mystery of life to our own frozen horizons, God patiently stretched us upward to ever-new frontiers of Divine Wisdom, opening new vistas of what is possible and necessary for living in the fullness of our divine/human potential.

With the wisdom that subverts and dismantles our stubborn efforts to create a god of our own image, to construct a society and religion to suit our own feeble reckoning of what is good, The Divine Trickster topples our expectations, demolishes our dreams of the Messianic era.

In one fell swoop the temple, the priesthood, the law, and self-serving dreams of messianic power are swept aside into impotent irrelevancy. Herod, the palace, all the royal prerogatives are reduced to a murderous, sputtering rage. A virgin, a powerless disenfranchised woman, a rag-tag band of unkempt, unrighteous, rowdy and despised shepherds, and foreigners from a distant land beyond the pale of Israel's salvation become the nobility of this upside-down kingdom. The reign of God enters history, becomes poor human flesh born in a cave, recognized and accepted by the outcasts of society, destined to wind up on a cross of shame, failure and powerlessness. This is the

God to whom we are asked to lend our flesh. This is the church, the Mystical Body, through which we seek to proclaim and make present in power the eternal Word of promise and salvation for all creation. This is what it means to be a people bonded together in a community we call the Body of Christ. We, the members of this body, are the womb into which the living God unceasingly impregnates the Word of life to become flesh throughout history, to take on the configuration of our body/spirit self, to be present in our presence, active, creative, redemptive by our willing participation in the mystery of divine life. To open our mind and heart to this God is indeed hazardous to the stability of our worldview. Properly understood, prayer frees us from uncritical loyalty to, and acceptance of, values and institutions that consciously or unconsciously diminish or inhibit our progress towards inner personal authority and responsible action. This is the mystery we seek to enter when we open ourselves in the action we call prayer. Is it any wonder so few risk it?

Hazardous though it be, with all the risks to our sense of security and well-being, it is what will pick our poor sick world up and turn it again towards the realization of the reign of Divine Wisdom already established among us, waiting to be released from the prison of our frightened hearts.

Chapter 3

Prayer: Uniting Heaven and Earth

When we look beyond theology, form, ritual and law for an understanding of the practice of prayer, we discover that our Judeo-Christian heritage conveys a deep and powerful experience of humanity's fundamental openness to the Divine, and the Divine urge towards union with humanity. Properly understood, we may say that prayer is our participation in the ongoing *kenosis* of God's self-emptying love. Human history, the events of individual lives being realized and coming to fruition in time, is the arena within which this union takes place. Prayer is a surrender to this most basic Divine/human imperative, a "yes" to our deeply-felt need for union with the Divine, a "let it be done" to the Divine overture to be united with us.

Blessed Isaac of Stella uses graphic images of pregnancy when speaking to his monks about the fruits of prayer. "May the Son of God who is formed in you grow strong and immense in you and become for you great gladness and exultation and perfect joy." (Bl. Isaac of Stella, 12th-century Cistercian abbot). The feminine image of prayer as pregnancy might be startling to our sensitivities accustomed to macho images of power and control. For all the difficulties involved however, it remains imperative for men as well as women to recognize the necessity of passivity with action, submission with engagement, the power of powerlessness, the fulfillment of emptiness.

Abraham and Sarah, Moses and the prophets, Mary and the apostles are the figures through which we apprehend this mystery of Divine/human engagement realized through the cooperation of historical human lives. Each in their own way confronted the mysteries, the imponderables surrounding and impinging upon their sense of meaning and purpose in the rush of historical events. Using these historical images as a base, we come to an understanding of prayer and its function in our lives.

As so often happens in the religious realm, thoughtless, uncritical acceptance of theological formulas or conventional expectations leads to mindless repetition and empty practice. This taxes our resources of time and personal energy without a corresponding restoration. The practice of prayer becomes a mere vestige of the truth, carried along on the crutch of compulsive adherence to law and formula or cultural religious conventions. Prayer becomes one more anxiety-producing, guilt-ridden burden imposed on an already-anxious, guilt-ridden existence. Under these circumstances, the practice of prayer often gives way to a self-justifying increase of enervating work in order to reduce the guilt of not praying. This ploy allows one to maintain a vestige of religious propriety. "I am too busy . . ." "I am too tired . . ." "My people, my family, my job put too many demands on me . . ." becomes the litany of one who has lost contact with the life-giving recreative energy of a personal encounter and relationship with the God who continually unfolds and deepens life.

Perhaps worse, the formalities of prayer can be coopted into the service of our hungry, ego-seeking affirmation for a self-righteous virtue masking our unresolved inner emptiness. Even our God-given hunger for wholeness can be a trap when the ego is not drawn into a transforming and purifying relationship with the Word. Prayer can become a personal turf where one's ego reigns supreme, unassailable and impregnable to all outside interventions and influences.

The devastation of inauthentic prayer, or prayer that dies under the weight of too many self-imposed professional, cultural or ministerial "urgencies," is incalculable. Instead of being energized by new possibilities, the human spirit is narcotized by the trivialization of prayer. One is deluded into a false sense of security and well-being, a false sense of being right with God, even as relationships, compassion, a prophetic sense of justice, and zeal for ministry diminish and finally disappear. Ministry with all its tasks and responsibilities becomes routinized and, like our prayer, coopted by the ego. Prayer and public worship become conveniently organized and programmed into tidy spaces where they are allowed as little as possible to intrude into zones of personal comfort. Inauthentic prayer so anesthetizes the spirit that one can live wrapped in a false sense of personal security, encapsulated in a safe space where "god" and the individual dwell together in mutual admiration. Prayer, instead of being an opening of the mind and heart to God, becomes a series of self-serving rituals closing the mind and heart on themselves. Ultimately the heart becomes sealed off, the mind closed, becoming one's personal kingdom, insulated from divine as well as human intrusions.

The first universal and essential element of authentic prayer found in all our models is openness. To be open before the mystery of the Divine is to accept and acknowledge our spiritual poverty. To open (raise) our mind and heart to God is to accept the reality of the limits and boundaries to our knowledge and understanding, as well as to our efforts.

To be open is to be receptive, vulnerable. It is to accept the possibility of a relationship with a dynamic other with all the changes that a relationship entails. There is an element of passivity, a willingness to be worked on, to be modified or changed. This attitude might not be conscious or fully articulated; however, all of our models were subsequently drawn into situations and tasks that they had not fully envisioned or willed. In prayer our defenses are down and we are open to receive new information that might cause us to change, to modify our present knowledge and behavior. In short, we open ourselves to become that which we had not previously thought we could become, to do that which we had not considered it possible for us to do, to believe what we never thought it possible to believe.

Our chosen models all shared a common willingness to listen, to move beyond previously-perceived limitations, to confront and resist tyrannical structures and cultural assumptions about roles and functions of men and women in society or church. They were able to respond to alternative ways of acting in a given set of circumstances. They got in touch with deeper realities, and new options, in circumstances that others had grown accustomed to and accepted as their lot. They did that which they would not have chosen to do, they went where they would not have chosen to go, believed in what they never dared believe in, namely a God who was free of temple ritual and human laws. They learned to believe in a God who called the chosen people to be free and responsible under the guidance of Divine Wisdom.

The soul of Mary of Nazareth exulted in the awareness that God's promise could and would be fulfilled in her. She intuited that because of the new life in her, the self-styled mighty with all their power would be toppled (Lk. 1:46-55). Elizabeth's salutation to her should echo in our hearts, saluting all who dare to believe that those promises made by God to the people can continue to be fulfilled in them (Lk.1:45). A person grounded in an understanding of God's desire to be one with us in prayer will not hesitate to proclaim with Mary: "The Lord has done great things in me." Through our prayer the Church, by means of individuals opening their hearts to God, continues to be the womb in which God takes on flesh and action in history. We boldly believe that God can do mighty things in our lives because we are God's creation. Faith means that when we say we believe in God, we are able to act as if we believe in ourselves.

There is a most striking illustration of this bold freedom in Luke's story of Martha and Mary. We know that Jewish convention in the time of Jesus was quite clear on the role of women. The men were the teachers, the carriers of tradition. The women were simply irrelevant and inconsequential in these areas. We can only imagine the astonishment and scandal that ensued as Mary boldly took her place at the feet of Jesus to participate in his wisdom. Even more scandalous was Jesus' refusal to send her packing back to the kitchen (Lk. 10:38-42).

What is important here is that we get no indication that Jesus invited Mary. It was Mary who sensed in herself a readiness and a capacity to explore new possibilities within herself. Jesus affirmed and welcomed this personal stretching into unfamiliar territory. While this is a model for all who awaken to new possibilities, we might also see it as a model for responding to the emerging roles of women in the Church. Jesus did not see himself as the custodian and guardian of human tradition, even those traditions believed to bear the authority of Moses, but rather saw himself as the "midwife" of emerging self-awareness. As Mary "woke up" and responded to her own deeply-felt intuitions, Jesus simply acknowledged and welcomed this awakening.

In Mary of Bethany, our biblical myth presents us with an image of the explosive power of a contemplative heart awakening to new depths of the meaning of life and action. In Mary a creative surge of life flows into bold action, enabling her to bore a hole in the wall of conventional religious and cultural stereotypes. Today as women—and men—awaken to the possibility of new roles and functions previously closed to them, Church leadership might be well-advised to model their responses on Christ, the midwife of new consciousness. If church and religious leaders could find the courage to replace the craven fear of innovation with trust in the innate goodness of the human person, the church community could reclaim its rightful place as the teacher and mother of new life, the bold pioneer of new possibilities for humanity and creation. In unambiguous fidelity to the law of Divine Wisdom, incarnate in Christ, the church community will be a sign of hope in the nobility of humanity and the restoration of its proper role in the evolution of creation.

In all of our biblical models we find examples of God's Word, eternally sent, finding fertile soil in hearts and minds opened to the Good News of new possibilities for humanity. The restoration of this union of divinity with humanity reestablishes the law of Divine Wisdom as the guiding principle of human action and the historical process.

Our traditional formula of prayer, properly understood, describes a process through which our minds and hearts, all minds and hearts through the sweep of history, are drawn into a personal encounter with the living, creative power of God's divine love, poured out through the Word. The fruit of our prayer takes us beyond ritual, law, formula, sacred times and places to a direct meeting with the Lord of all time and space. Through prayer our limited time and place is opened and filled with the eternal Divine. We become our prayer, we become the temple suffused with God's eternal presence. Our entire being becomes a manifestation of God's sovereign rule present in compassion, a thirst for justice, human energy invested in the building of the reign of Holy Wisdom. Prayer transforms the mind and heart so that our actions become sacramental actions mediating Divine Wisdom.

In Acts, St. Luke uses a creative literary device to illustrate his understanding of the transmission of Christ's mission across the chasm of his death to the community of disciples. In the lives of the members of the community, the Holy Spirit takes up residence and continues the saving work of Jesus, even to miracles, trials and persecutions. The same power operative in Jesus now flows into history through the lives of the resurrection community. Jesus is not just another historical figure, a political and religious zealot whose word and message live on in some romanticized story. Jesus is seen as the one whose living spirit and action took possession of history through previously-weak human agents. The movements of the disciples, particularly Paul and Peter, are really understood to be the movement of God's Word. In our lives in a faithful community, we are called to be the dwelling place of divine power confronting alienated egocentric power seeking to establish its own self-serving reign.

Luke likewise uses Stephen to link the ongoing life of the community to Jesus. In Stephen's trial the charges brought against Jesus are now leveled at Stephen. Namely that Stephen, like Jesus, attacked the temple and the law. As in Jesus' trial, so too in Stephen's, false witnesses come forth to testify that he predicted that the temple would be destroyed, this time by Jesus. Later the same accusations would be made against Paul. Perhaps it is not too great a stretch of the imagination to believe that the apostolic community saw itself as a challenge to the tyranny of religious forces coopted into the service of human interests. When the Spirit of God possesses a person or a community, there are inevitable conflicts with established interests. Measured against the standard of the Acts of the Apostles, the church was never intended to be a quiet and docile presence in human affairs. Nor were persons seen as passive spectators in the affairs of this prophetic community.

Luke is teaching the community that if the Word of God as taught by Jesus was to have the same power, then like Jesus, the disciples would have to face the same kind of persecutions and trials. The community of disciples, and later the church, was to be in every way the body of Christ.

Luke skillfully uses Stephen's death to link the community of Acts to the mission of Jesus. Like Jesus, Stephen is arrested and executed as one who subverts the authority of the Church and its political allies. Like Jesus, Stephen dies peacefully praying for his executioners, but at his death, he looks to heaven and there sees the glorious Christ at the right hand of God (Acts 7:55-60).

What more clear and dramatic indication could we find of the community's self-identity after the Resurrection/Pentecost event? Clearly, the community saw itself as the dwelling place of the Holy Spirit, their own lives and actions as being the sacrament whereby Christ continued living and acting in history, bringing about a new humanity, a new creation. Through the community, the Word of God would be released from the law and the temple to spread throughout the world to all the ends of the earth. In this we have a theme repeated throughout our salvation myth: the Power of God's Word being brought about by the coming of the Holy Spirit is inseparable from the cooperation of human instruments. Just as God's Word became incarnate in Mary through the Spirit, so the Spirit of God continues to bring about the incarnation of the Word in the body of Christ, men and women. Bringing about the reign of compassionate justice, the triumph of Divine Wisdom over human folly, is a Divine-human enterprise.

Throughout history the Word continues to be sent into the darkness and void of our own chaos, the confusion of our unenlightened hearts to bring order, truth, beauty and harmony to our time and place. Each of us is called in the tradition of Abraham and Sarah, Moses and the Prophets, Mary and the apostles, the saints, mystics and prophets of our own time to be open before God. We are challenged to be still in the Divine presence, to attend and respond to the silent whisper of new possibilities, even within the discouraging and disheartening confusion of our day.

Together as a community of prayer we are the womb through which the chaos and confusion of our world receives the seed of new life. Individually and corporately we are a womb capable of being impregnated with new opportunity for the Divine Word to continue finding flesh. Prayer is a surrender of our lives to the divine initiative seeking to take on the configuration of our body, mind and spirit to redeem and heal history, continuing the work that was begun when God said: "Let there be . . ."

Chapter 4

Sermon on the Mount:
A Restored Humanity

It is interesting to note that unlike the Buddha, or teachers of other traditions, Jesus did not give detailed instructions on the discipline of prayer. We hear nothing of postures, techniques, emphasis on controlling thoughts or emotions. He did caution against "standing in synagogues and on street corners to be seen by men" (Mt. 6:5), "babbling" (Mt. 6:7) as if we had to instruct God in detail about our needs, the needs of the world and how God should address these needs. Significant is the statement that God knows our needs before we ask for them (Mt. 6:8). Jesus seems to indicate that prayer is more an intimate and personal matter of the heart, of opening our heart to the heart of God.

In Matthew's Gospel we gain some insight into Jesus' understanding of prayer from the fact that his teaching occurs within the framework of the Sermon on the Mount, a development of the revelation given to the Israelites at Sinai. Sinai marks a turning point, imparting a new sense of what it means to be human and covenanted to a God living and acting in history, transforming relationships.

What is often overlooked in contemporary spiritual and moral theology is that to live according to God's law is to live according to the innate truth of woman and man. It is to live according to the divine truth out of which creation and humanity were spoken into existence. God beheld the work of Divine Wisdom and pronounced it very good (Gen. 1:31). The mystic poets of our myth imagine a time when man and woman reflected the pure beauty of God's eternal truth. This truth was most clearly manifest by the transparent intimacy shared between Adam and Eve; their nakedness was not an embarrassment, not a cause for covering themselves in shame and the fear of being known (Gen. 2:21- 25). This unembarrassed intimacy and unprotected presence to the other characterized their relationship to creation and ultimately to God. We have been created for union with God; only in union with God do we fully realize the truth of our nature. As we make our way through our shared story from Genesis through the Christian Covenant, we discover that this is also the story of our shared destiny.

The "happy fault" that we celebrate in liturgy is none other than the moment in which we arrive at a point of self-awareness that brings with it the capacity to make choices. We have the ability to choose our bliss or our damnation. Sin is the price we pay and the risk we take in being free. Our path to holiness, to full humanity, takes us through the perilous regions of sin and error. To seek to avoid the risks of freedom is to fail in the challenge capable of bringing us to the fullness of humanity.

Sin severs union with God; but sin also alienates us from the truth of ourselves created in the divine image (Gen. 3). The Law given on Sinai is the law that was first written in our hearts, that continues in our hearts, driving us on an insatiable search to recapture and possess the union from which we have been severed, the union with God that is also union with the truth of our individual selves, created to show forth the beauty and truth of God. It is helpful to note here that our natural inclination is not toward sin but toward truth, unity with the source and end of all truth. Sin is the search for unity and truth snagged on the broken edges of our alienated ego. The Law of Sinai awakens us to the faint echo of truth deep within our hearts. To live in sin, to commit sin, is to offend against our God-like dignity; it is to taint the wisdom of God's inner truth of which we are the most perfect reflection.

The Sermon on the Mount takes the Law given to Moses to its ultimate conclusion. It charts the perilous journey through our encounter with sin to union with the heart of God. This union is a reconstitution of authentic personhood in freedom, unembarrassed, undefended intimacy with humanity, creation and God. It draws out in detail the task of purification from bondage to our alienated ego to the utter freedom exemplified by Christ on the cross. It is a charter for a renewed humanity restored to the original truth from which it was created. Jesus on the cross is the image of the human person freed from the tyranny of the egocentric self, free to love as God loves. The crucified Jesus is the image of the person totally emptied of all that is not true and holy, emptied of the fear and suspicion we have for one another, filled with the fullness of God's life. Jesus on the cross is the paradigm of a humanity restored to its original state of total union with uncreated love.

The Sermon on the Mount has its foundations in the journey of Christ into the wilderness to encounter the satanic forces that tear and divide the heart and set us at odds with ourselves, one another and creation. The unfortunate tendency of our Western scientific mind is to attempt to concretely historicize our myth. We are left with a comedic trivialization of the figure of Satan which few, if any, take seriously. The evangelists had a much more serious and dramatic encounter in mind than later folk piety and theologizing manages to convey. In this episode, Jesus encounters a very real and frightening power that lives in each one of us and subtly rules our values and subsequent decisions. Through Jesus' wilderness episode, the evangelists seek to warn us to be on the alert against these forces, and like Jesus, identify and repudiate their influence in our lives. Through this personal identification of the power of sin in our lives, we can then continue the journey to the Mountain of Beatitudes.

We cannot fully understand the Sermon, nor can we grasp the Lord's Prayer in all its depth unless we see them as issuing from the encounter in the wilderness. It often comes as a shock to the pious that the first function of the Holy Spirit of God is to lead the Savior into an encounter with evil. The temptations illustrate for us the seductive enticements that delude us into easy gratifications of the innate hunger of the soul that is at the same time our hunger for spiritual fullness.

How seductively innocent is the search for bread, survival, the preservation of life! Yet we see all around us the cruelty, destruction and evil that accompany the unrestrained, egocentric pursuit of the necessities of life. When personhood is experienced in isolation to other persons, we are at war. We live as adversaries, in competition for the scarce commodities of the earth.

War begins in the heart, nourished by a justifiable need to survive and provide for loved ones, tribe, clan or nation, even at the cost of the lives of other persons, families, tribes or nations. Into this equation Christ inserts the Word of God (Mt. 4:4). Agape, the love of a sister for her brother, a parent for a child, a friend for a friend becomes the mitigating factor in the primitive, unrestrained pursuit of personal survival. Eucharist, sharing one's table, the fruits of one's labor, surrendering body and blood in love of neighbor becomes the mark of a consciousness transformed by the Christ event ocurring within the heart. The rigid defensive boundaries of the self are stretched to include the entire human family; the mind and heart of Christ become incarnate in human flesh. The Incarnation continues through history. Liberation from the tyranny of war begins within individual hearts who allow the power of the eucharistic symbol to become the ground from which their life extends into transformed relationships.

In the second temptation, Christ exposes the face of Evil lurking in the heart of one who would serve God and then expect God to ratify and cooperate with the presumptions of our unredeemed and unenlightened consciousness. Not the power of the temple, but God alone do we serve. Our claim on God's divine favor rests on the ground of our willingness to let God be God. We do not diminish God's wisdom and sovereignty to our dwarfed dimensions and self-serving agendas (Mt. 4:7). Christ is free from the allurements of a temple religion grown complacent and shallow in the self-serving assurances and unreflective arrogance that assume that our corporate will is God's will. The cross on a hill of shame and failure, weakness and poverty of spirit is the occasion of God's frightening breakthrough into history. The earth quakes at the scandal of seeing failure and humiliation, weakness and spiritual poverty, a seeming abandonment even by God, replace the pomp of temple and the arrogance of human self-righteousness through law. The heart of God, one with the broken heart of Christ, reaches beyond priests, Pharisees, Sadducees and kings to become one with the broken, tattered heart of humanity. Dismas the criminal, Mary the prostitute, tax collectors, Gentile wisemen with disenfranchised and no-account women, and unwashed rowdies are the royalty in the Kingdom of this subversive loser hanging, writhing on a criminal's cross. What a striking indictment of much of Christianity's present-day leadership who consider these images to be objects of theological study and speculation, thus safely blunting their impact on their daily life and practice.

In the third temptation to political power we are reminded that history is all too full of futile attempts to unite the authority of heaven with that of politics. In the attempt, God and divine wisdom become appropriated into the service of human sinfulness. Examples abound of human suffering and tragedy perpetrated under the banner of God's authority superimposed on the name of a king or president, pope, bishop, priest, or president of a parish council. Christ peered into the face of the Evil One and exposed the liar lurking in the crevasses beneath our noble motives to bring political power and prestige into the service of gods created in our image. Christ, incarnate wisdom, repudiated and turned from such audacity (Mt. 4:10). Knowing the pain of the human heart with its insatiable lust for the easy way, Christ turned us to the tortuous task of radical purification and emptying. He knows what lies beneath the layers of egotistical defenses against powerlessness and nonviolence: the very brilliance of God's own divine image.

Refreshed, liberated, with the clear vision of a new humanity, a new creation beginning in the renewed hearts of man and woman, one heart at a time, he climbed the Mountain of Beatitude to proclaim and announce a new epoch for humanity, a new direction for history. He confounded and confused, angered and dismayed many by his repudiation of everything that seemed so normal, so wise and so innocent. He set foot on the path of folly, revealing divine wisdom hidden, lost, long-forgotten in the deep recesses of the human heart.

That same path begins for us when we, like the apostles in Luke's Gospel, ask: "Lord, teach us to pray" (Lk. 11:1). We are taught the prayer that is already buried deep in our hearts waiting for us to release it into our lives. "Our Father in heaven, holy be *your* name, may *your* kingdom come, may *your* will be done on earth as it is in heaven."

Prayer is much more than postures and breathing, devotions and obligations, candles and monstrances. It is the opening of our deepest self to be taken, transformed and sent as a sacrament of God's divine love given to all.

Chapter 5

The Heart:
Dwelling Place of the Word

The author of the letter to the Hebrews repeats, mantra-like, his plea: open your hearts, soften them, be attentive, receive God's word, be present. "As the Holy Spirit says: if only you would listen to him today! Do not harden your hearts, as at the rebellion . . ." (Heb 3:7). "Take care . . . that none of you ever has a wicked heart, so unbelieving as to turn away from the living God" (Heb. 3:12). "If only you would listen to him today; do not harden your hearts as at the rebellion" (Heb 3:15). There is a sense of urgency. It is imperative that God's word be attended to. The Word is sent, like the sunshine, the air, the rain; we dare not cover ourselves, insulate ourselves from its life-sustaining influence. We are reminded again that it is a matter of a listening heart, a heart freed from the bondage to unenlightened preoccupations that burden and afflict without offering life.

There is the faint outline of the catechism definition inviting us to surrender our deepest self to be possessed by God's presence, God's wisdom and power. Our lives are not to be lived in a distant, disconnected relationship with a void between ourselves and the Divine. We are promised intimacy: lives fused and commingled as one. The liturgy of the Eucharist celebrates this audacious hope each time the priest prepares to offer the bread and the wine: "By the mystery of this water and wine may we come to share in the divinity of Christ, who humbled himself to share in our humanity" (Offertory).

One of the most extraordinary passages in Scripture is in the letter to the Ephesians (3:14-19). Paul emphasizes the dynamic, active presence in power of Christ in our inner being growing strong through faith that we may be filled to the measure of all the fullness of God.

Scripture gives us every assurance that God's power is available to us. However, we determine the quality and depth of our relationship with the Divine One. Matthew 6:5 speaks of prayer coming from the heart of one who uses it as a means of winning social approval. In 6:7 he describes a heart intent on overwhelming God with a barrage of words: magic prayer, the prayer of a manipulative, insecure heart, a heart afraid to surrender and entrust one's needs into the hands of a lover.

Our prayer is not above scrutiny. We dare not take it for granted and assume that just because we go through the motions everything will fall into line. Our relationship with God, and prayer is the ground of that relationship, is subject to the same distortions and self-serving manipulations as any other relationship. Prayer will reflect the quality of our own self understanding, our ability to let go and allow ourselves to be taken by another. If allowed to grow and flourish, prayer, like any relationship, will take us to new and unexpected levels of self-knowledge affording us the opportunity to change, to become more true, authentic and simple in the presence of the other. But first, we need to let go of control, the need to be in charge, to make things happen our way.

One of the major problems with prayer today is that we have grown distrustful of our sacred, divinely-authored uniqueness, the sacred subjectivity of our own experience of life and the divine presence and action in our life. We constantly look to others for approval and ratification. Thus, we ignore or make light of our need to respond from our own deep center where the divine and human intersect, commingle in a unity of divine love and our unique, personal, human need. We judge our prayer according to external standards of performance. We think we know what we need and how God should answer our requests. Prayer as a process of entering into the realm of the unfolding mystery of our unique being, where the unexpected and even unwanted might happen, is foreign to many of us.

In Hebrews 4:12-13, the author is clear and unambiguous in stating the radical relationship between a person and the Word of God. It is the Word that is active and dynamic, not the one receiving it. It is the person who is acted upon, opened at the deepest layers of being, laid bare, revealed and known. It is not we who lay hold of the mystery of the Word, but rather it is we who surrender ourselves to be scrutinized, interpreted, known, and judged by the Wisdom of God's Word. Through the Word we are enlarged and transformed, raised to union with God. "The word of God is something alive and active: it cuts more incisively than any two-edged sword: it can seek out the place where soul is divided from spirit, or joints from marrow; it can pass judgement on secret emotions and thoughts. No created thing is hidden from him; everything is uncovered and stretched fully open to the eyes of the one to whom we must give account of ourselves" (Heb 4:12-13 NJB). The similarity between this passage and our catechism definition is inescapable: we lift, open, surrender our mind and heart to God.

Examining again the images of our biblical models, we recognize Abraham and Sarah, Moses and the prophets as examples of persons caught and possessed at the deepest level of their personhood. From deep within their being they were awakened and raised to unexpected heights of human possibility, thrust into a hair-raising adventure with life as an alternative to the deadening routine of slavery. Likewise we remember Mary and her prayer of response to the messenger of the Lord: Behold the servant, the expectant one, the empty and humble one. "'Let it happen to me as you have said . . .'"(Lk. 1:38 NJB). And so she began that harrowing and courageous journey leading her to be the woman of sorrows at the foot of a cross of shame. Mary is the most dramatic and uncompromising model of one truly caught and possessed by the Word. It impregnated her and became one with her flesh, spilled out of her into an impoverished and waiting world, leading her to be the woman of sorrows clutching the dead and mutilated body of that Word that had taken her flesh and drew her into the mystery of God's redemptive plan. It is no accident that the Church early on recognized her as the model of church. You and I are that church, each in our own lives, called to make that mystery present in our generation. What a radical repudiation of much that passes for prayer today: manipulative, self-centered, seeking to reduce God and the sovereign will to our petty dimensions and egocentric agendas.

Unapologetically our biblical tradition of prayer calls us to forget ourselves, our self-centered preoccupation with our agendas. We are invited to surrender to Divine Wisdom, to be opened to a wider and deeper perception of reality. Through prayer we are released from the time-bound, hide-bound limitations of our egocentric perceptions. The choice is clear: to be transformed, enlightened and enlarged by Divine Wisdom, or to impose our limited perceptions on God, to seek to draw God into our manipulative agendas and wind up with a false god created in our own dwarfed image and likeness. Many of us live with a God no larger, no more powerful than our own theologically-imposed definitions. All too many have allowed theology, law and ritual ceremony to become a substitute for the earthquake, fire and wind of God's living presence in power. Thus, in the place of bold prophetic action, a courageous mystical vision, a contemplative heart faithfully attentive to the voice of God in history, we find cynicism, discouragement, anger and confusion as we beat against the walls of our own self-imposed prisons.

When we come into the presence of the Divine with wonder, expectation, awe and curiosity, like a wind rushing into a vacuum, the Word will penetrate our heart to take possession of history, to continue the divine creative work of bringing order to chaos, light to darkness, life where before there was emptiness and death. What are perceived by many to be moments of loss and failure, impotence and rage become transformed into occasions for the release of creative prophetic energy. Our heart, though burdened with anger at injustice, weighted down with sorrow at human tragedy and blind absurdity, is moved by a stubborn belief that this is not the end of the story. We are a people pierced and opened by a vision of a new possibility for humanity and creation. We refuse to be seduced by the lie of conventional cultural wisdom. Prayer is the celebration of our life responding to a fundamental openness to the Divine, to be transformed into a sacrament of God's presence in power bringing history to its appointed end, even as we experience the power and forces of sin raging around us.

"If only you would listen to him today, do not harden your hearts . . ." Dare we admit to ourselves that perhaps inadvertently, ever so slowly and subtly, the contemplative, the mystical and the prophetic dimensions of our tradition, those elements so deeply rooted in the heart center, have been taken over and replaced by logic, the tidiness of orthodox theology, the regularity, predictability, and control of temple worship. A word intended to take root in the heart has been replaced by a religion that has seized power over our minds and wills, diminishing human possibility rather than opening our horizons to the outermost reaches of human possibility transformed in love. Jesus' nonviolent response to evil, his obedient surrender into the Father's hands, Mary's silent and humble "let it be done . . ." have shaken the earth, toppled powers, exalted the humble, as testimony to what can and must happen when hearts are courageous and bold enough to surrender to the God of history.

Honesty will require us to acknowledge a need for conversion on the part of many who are called to lead others in prayer.

The basic law of prayer requires us to acknowledge that, for us, words, gestures, times and places contain no magic power to mediate the divine and open the mind and heart to God. True prayer in our tradition requires an initial openness to a relationship with a personal God whose unique self-expression we are. To open ourselves to this relationship is to submit to being drawn into the unfolding mystery of our true human potential. It is the unhampered, free and creative development of the person that reveals God's Divine Image and power in history in a unique way.

In this process we are drawn away from delusion and sham, the sham of our own shallow perceptions and egocentric desires. Prayer is a surrender to a confrontation with the lies and darkness of the false self that we have mistakenly believed to be the true self. To open ourselves to truth, Jesus Christ, the eternal Word, is at the same time to open ourselves to the realization of everything that is false in our lives. If prayer is surrendering the heart to be drawn into the light of Divine Wisdom, the triumph of love in time, it is also the beginning of a journey into the wilderness to face the Evil One and the subtle and unrecognized tyranny of sin in our everyday lives.

Surrendering the heart and mind to prayer, submitting to the two-edged sword that is God's living word, can be a frightening experience before we begin to get a firmer glimpse of the reality of the truth and possibility that is the true ground of our existence. Is it any wonder that we have been so creative in finding less troubling alternatives?

   "If today you hear God's voice . . ."

Chapter 6

The Enemy:
Brother and Sister Before God

On the matter of prayer, Jesus makes a point of emphasizing the need to rid the heart of any barrier between ourselves and others. In this teaching, the notion of forgiveness of enemies holds a paramount place. "So then, if you are bringing your offering to the altar and there remember that your brother has something against you, leave your offering there before the altar, go and be reconciled with your brother first, and then come back and present your offering" (Mt. 5:23-24 NJB). As we seek to ground ourselves in the values of the Gospel and open ourselves to the reign of God in our hearts, we will be confronted by our enemies holding the key that will enable us to continue on our journey. Our enemy is an essential element, a vital part of our membership in the reign of Holy Wisdom and our ultimate union with God, Abba. "But I say this to you, love your enemies and pray for those who persecute you; so that you may be children of your Father in heaven, for he causes his sun to rise on the bad as well as the good, and sends down rain to fall on the upright and the wicked alike." ". . . You must set no bounds to your love, just as your heavenly Father sets none to his" (Mt 5:44-45;48 NJB).

The figure of the enemy stands as a sign of the ultimate tyranny over the heart. The enemy represents the definitive challenge in the quest for freedom and the unassailable peace of the reign of Divine Love. Long after we have distanced ourselves from the presence and erosive influence of the enemy, long after we may have outdone, even outlived the enemy, he or she will continue to insinuate their presence into our innermost thoughts and deepest memories. The continuing erosive influence of anger and resentment, laced with self-pity, continues to eat away at our lives and endeavors, souring our spirit. We cannot be right with ourselves or with God until we make peace with our enemy. The enemy stands on our path to the altar, demanding that we release our heart from the grip of resentment. The gift of ourselves to God is taken to the altar by the one who has wounded us to the core.

As mentioned above, prayer is the process whereby we open our deepest self to God to be probed and known; it is a willingness to be possessed and known by the Divine at the deepest level. When the true self is hidden from consciousness, layered over by the defensive maneuvers of denial, minimizing, or avoidance, we cannot be opened to surrender to the God who pours love on all. How can we expect to be united to God when our love is fenced in by the selective limitations of our outraged ego? When we love only those who love us in return, are we not asking that God relate to us on our terms, within our diminished dimensions? We attempt to force God to comply to our restricted perceptions of reality rather than surrendering to the transforming and enlarging power of the Spirit. Only through such a surrender can we grow into the truth of our human potential to be like God. Otherwise, the living God who desires to be united with us in our everyday lives and relationships is replaced by a plastic god who accepts our self-serving pieties and legalistic devotions, while requiring no significant change on our part. By the very nature of our self-protective ego, our fear of our own darkness, the shame of our participation in the sin and violence of the human family, our enemy is the one who is most able to cut us to the quick, to lay us open at the center and reveal to us the dark and unredeemed hidden self, the self we so strenuously seek to hide, not only from others with whom we live, but ourselves and even God. If we find ourselves wondering why our prayer seems so superficial, so fleeting in its healing effects, perhaps we should search our deep hearts to see if we are not cherishing some deep wound, anger, rage or petty resentment. In our day of pop psychology and the proliferation of bland and serendipitous religious practices, it is all too easy to believe we can get away with harboring our petty, and not so petty, grievances at the indignities suffered at the hands of others.

Why is the Christian consciousness haunted by the cross and the awesome spectacle of the Christ calling down forgiveness on the enemies who were taking not only possessions, but the last shred of dignity and life as well? Having life wrenched from us is the ultimate insult to one's sense of purpose, one's meaning and value. Execution, assassination, murder, the deprivation of life for the convenience of others, is the ultimate and radical annihilation of the last shred of human dignity. One is deemed expendable; life is brushed aside as if no more significant than a pesky mosquito. If ever there seemed to be a justification for rage and retaliation, for fighting violence with violence, it would appear to be in the defense of one's life, one's mission and vision for a better world. But no! The God who became like us in order to reveal the forgotten glory of our true nature chooses to forgive those who intrude into the divine plan, taking matters into their own hands in order to put their agenda in the place of divine wisdom.

It is a paradox of the spiritual life that the one most likely to help us in prayer is our enemy, the one who lays us open to the the dark, unredeemed corners of our deepest soul. The one who wounds us most deeply is the one we must invite to accompany us on the journey to meet the face of the living God waiting to be revealed in that deepest self where we so often fear to travel.

The Christian person is uncompromisingly confronted with the disconcerting reality of Christ's command to "take up the cross . . ." We are not allowed to avert our gaze from the writhing, suffering one forgiving his murderers, forgiving and continuing to embrace those intimate friends abandoning him even as he suffers and commends his spirit to the Heavenly Mother-Father, the womb of Divine Wisdom. Christ, the sinless one, the first-born of the new creation, is the one who passed through sin and stopped it dead in its tracks by receiving hatred, violence, human pettiness into his sinless soul, transforming it, and releasing it as unconditional love.

Contrary to much conventional spirituality today, there is no other way for us to follow Christ. There is no way to evade the clarity of the command and the direction of the road we must follow. The cross stands on our path as surely as it stood in the destiny of Christ and his disciples. Prayer is none other than a stance of openness, of readiness to enter the journey. For prayer to continue to grow and develop, to enlarge us and open us to union with the Divine Life of God, it needs to be planted and rooted in our willingness to forgive and embrace the enemy as brother and sister. Paradoxically, the one we most fear, the one we would most eagerly avoid or count as insignificant, is the one who holds the key to our progress; our enemy is the messenger who reveals to us the area of our life impeding our journey to union with the divine, the radical opening of our deepest self to be possessed and transformed by the victory of Christ.

To understand the true nature of prayer, to grasp the dramatic and intense encounter to which we open ourselves, is to understand why it is so tempting and easy to replace it with trivial and self-serving sub-stitutes. To avoid prayer is to avoid not only an encounter with that part of our person most needing redemption and healing, it is to miss bringing to life the truest dimension of ourselves, the hidden self. The self where Divinity and humanity merge, commingle and become one in the fullness of human life, remains buried under the debris of fears, rationalizations, and pretenses.

To open ourselves to union with God is a surrender into the deepest truth of our human nature. We make a radical affirmation of the hid-den truth of ourselves created by the infinite goodness of God, destined and designed to show forth God-like qualities. Our relationship with God is a renewed relationship with ourselves. We make an act of faith in what God has done for us by loving and willing us into life, believ-ing with Mary that God will do marvelous things in us.

When Jesus invites us to take up the cross and follow after him, he is affirming the divinely-authored beauty of the human person and the goodness of creation. It is an invitation to surrender to the purification of divine love by submitting to the stripping away of all that is not good and holy in our lives and actions. It is an invitation to be awak-ened to the truth of our God-like qualities while seeing and being hum-bled by our shallowness, our narrowness and arrogance. As our narco-tized souls are awakened, we are confronted with the awesome and deadly reality of our self-deceptions, our self-serving maneuvers and manipulations even of holy things. At the same time we see the vision of what is coming to be in our soul, the promise and the potential being renewed by the Wisdom of God. We understand that we have been created for the sole purpose of radiating the love of God through the total giving of ourselves, body-soul-spirit. We realize that we have ap-propriated that thirst for selfish purposes; we have prostituted ourselves with false gods of our own making, subject to our willfulness. We un-derstand that Jesus is sent to reveal, not only the truth of the Divine

One, but at the same time the absolute and unshakable truth of humanity created in the Divine Image and participating in Divine goodness. Prayer is more than thoughts and words. It releases energy in concrete prophetic service, even to our enemies.

We awaken to the realization that our enemies are messengers sent to reveal and expose those areas of our hidden self where rage and fury lurk. We are led to that place in our hearts where we and the enemy are one, where the sin of humanity resides. We gasp in amazement as we realize that we stand beside our enemy before the cross being showered equally with divine love and forgiveness. We turn and face our enemy to embrace as brothers and sisters in the saving life of Christ. We come humbly to the altar bearing the wound of all humanity. In our soul, the transformation of sin into grace, hatred into love, violence into nonviolence continues. The mind and heart of Christ frees and transform the ego, enabling us to fully live the Christ-event, allowing the Christ-event to continue in our lives and relationships. With Paul, we pray: "I have been crucified with Christ and yet I am alive; yet it is no longer I, but Christ living in me . . ." (Gal. 2:19-20 NJB).

Life is no longer words spoken, but the Word lived; ministry no longer a series of segmented actions, but the sacrifice of Christ being completed in each action and every relationship. Prayer is no longer mere words said, but life lived from the depths. It does not separate us into sinners and saints, but welcomes us into a community of sinners celebrating redemptive love by the love we have for one another. The prayer of Paul to the Ephesians becomes a living reality pouring into the world through our individual lives joined in a bond of forgiving and being forgiven: "In the abundance of his glory may he, through his spirit, enable you to grow firm in power with regard to your inner self, so that Christ may live in your hearts through faith, and then, planted in love and built on love, with all God's holy people you will have the strength to grasp the breadth and the length, the height and the depth; so that, knowing the love of Christ, which is beyond knowledge, you may be filled with the utter fullness of God" (Eph. 3:16-19 NJB).

Chapter 7

Sabbath:
A Holy Place in the Heart

"Thus the heavens and the earth were completed in all their vast array.

"By the seventh day God had finished the work he had been doing; so on the seventh day he rested from all his work. And God blessed the seventh day and made it holy, because on it he rested from all the work of creating he had done" (Gen 2:1-3).

In this marvelously simple, almost naive imagery of God resting after the work of creation, the author invites us to meditate on the natural rhythm of action and rest, word and silence, the silence of wonder in the presence of the work accomplished. Divine rest allows creation its turn to speak and praise the worker to whom it owes existence. In the flow of action and repose, word and silence, creator and creation are engaged at a level of simple, mutual presence. There is reciprocity, an encounter of mutual participation in the mystery of being and becoming. In the words of Martin Buber, an "I—thou" relationship is established between the worker and the works. In silent repose a sense of reverence, of awe, emerges, allowing creation to be present in its inherent dignity to the creator. Creation is no longer simply an object, an "it," a thing "out there." It moves from being a mere "product" to become a subject endowed with dignity and purpose, calling for reverence and respect from the one to whom it owes existence. In resting, God allows creation to simply be, and in being, to draw attention to the dignity contained in the simple act of gratuitous existence. There is a sense that creative action is somehow completed in stillness, that words spoken reveal the true depths of their meaning when followed by "wonder-full" silence. Silent stillness enfolds unrealized meaning of act and word.

Silence and stillness are necessary moments of creation, every bit as dynamic and creative as action and words. We glimpse divine participation in the natural ebb and flow of action and stillness as a quality of the divine nature itself. Physical nature models for us an essential quality of divine and human nature.

In Exodus the observance of the Lord's Holy Day is codified and made mandatory for the people. "Remember the Sabbath day and keep it holy. For six days you shall labor and do all your work, but the seventh day is a Sabbath for Yahweh your God. You shall do no work that day, neither you nor your son nor your daughter nor your servants, men or women, nor your animals nor the alien living with you. . . ." And there is a reason given. "For in six days Yahweh made the heavens, earth, and sea, and all that these contain, but on the seventh day he rested. That is why Yahweh has blessed the Sabbath day and made it sacred" (Ex. 20:8-11 NJB). The sabbath rest is a holy space carved by the Creator into the flow of creation. It is a holy time to be still, to stand aside from the flow of events, the events unleashed by our own creative action, to remember our true place in the overall scheme of things. It is a time to remember that if we are creators, we have first been created.

Man and woman share in the creative work of God by guiding and nourishing the creative forces of divine wisdom. On the seventh day, now a day holy to the Lord, there is a cessation of work to bring balance to the six days of human labor in which chaos, darkness and emptiness continue to be drawn into order, beauty and life through human labor in partnership with divine wisdom. The work of order, beauty and life is balanced by the stillness and quiet of divine contemplation. In sabbath rest, man and woman contemplate and celebrate the sacred rhythm of creation within themselves. In shared repose, we glimpse a gentleness, a non-violence that softens the interaction between human and nonhuman creation. In labor we are divided into functions and roles; in silence and stillness, dominance and subservience, roles and functions cease as we take our common place, together with the work of our hands, before the majesty of the One from whom all life and existence come. Creation and the work of our hands are no longer object and product, but are freed from possessive ownership to simply be and reflect mutually-shared dignity in being. Men and women, created in the divine image, commanded to guide the unfolding of creation, cease their activity, rest and contemplate the works of their hands. As in God, so in creation; as in creation, so in man and woman, the rhythms of action into stillness, of word into silence must be held in sacred memory. In stillness there is germinating a seed of creative action, new beginnings; in silence germinates the seed of a creative word ready to continue the eternal utterance of divine wisdom through the evolution of creation. In man and woman the sacred rhythm of action and repose becomes the threshold through which creation and creator encounter and renew life in each other. New life, new beginnings flow from the small fragile space between action and rest, word and silence. The mystic poets of the Old Testament saw the nature of God manifested in creation. Thus, men and women were to realize their god-like responsibility in and for nature by consciously attending to the divine rhythms within themselves and celebrating these rhythms in their relationships with one another and creation. They dared not violate the holy rhythm within themselves and nature. On the seventh day they were to cease their action, contemplate and ponder the mysterious unfolding of creation and their participation within the unfolding divine plan. They were to remember that all creation owes its existence to the divine mother-father God self-revealing through creation. On this one day, men and women were to remember that they are always subservient to a wisdom and creative power greater than their own. To lose touch with that sacred rhythm is to lose touch with the precarious balance between isolated, egocentric, human action and God-centered action harmonized with, and flowing within the sacred rhythms of creation.

Separated from the sacred rhythm of creation, human action falls into its egocentric obsession with power unrelated to anything outside itself. Human power becomes self-absorbed, drawn into the tyranny of the isolated, inflated ego desirous only of establishing its consuming authority over all it surveys. Creation with all its life-giving power is reduced to an object, a commodity, an "it" without dignity or purpose other than to amuse, entertain and satisfy the rapacious greed of the empty human heart. The earth becomes ravaged under the relentless tyranny of men and women consumed by addiction to power and control, intoxicated by possessions wrenched from a seemingly un-complaining and gentle mother earth endlessly yielding her bounty. Material creation, humans, animals and plants are reduced to mere objects of manipulation and consumption.

Silently, subtly, like the insidious cell of a cancer relentlessly claiming its place in an unsuspecting body, human arrogance overrides our sense of place in creation and the evolution of the earth. The careful and reverential caring for the earth is replaced by greed, the addiction to possess and manipulate. The soul is consumed by a drive for personal power at the expense of life-giving energy in harmonious interaction with creation, other persons, animals and plants.

Soon, the fragile sacred place between silence and word, stillness and action is lost to our memory. Despised and maligned, feared and avoided, silence and stillness become desert places, wildernesses of the soul inhabited by the creatures of our nightmares. Silence becomes a curse, a frightful encounter with our inner emptiness, our impoverished spirit. Solitude becomes loneliness and spiritual desolation where we face our futility, the shallowness of endeavors beneath which lurks the specter of our mortality. Inactivity is seen as dreaded idleness to be avoided at all costs, lest we appear powerless, irrelevant and useless in a society that has turned action into a god blessing human endeavor for its own sake. Mortality and human weakness are experienced as affronts to our fragile sense of existence in a world replete with powers threatening to overwhelm us. We face our isolated, egocentric self shorn of its props and delusions of well-being and security. Terrified at the spector of our inner emptiness, we flee into frenzied action awash in the sounds of rootless words and empty gestures passing for relationships.

To lose our inner orientation, the fruit of holy silence and solitude, is to be cast adrift in a desert night without moon or stars to guide us. When men and women become intoxicated with achievements, when dreams are disconnected from the source and ground of the divine evolutionary scheme, we scamper about like panicky ants disrupted by the idle, mischievous, probing stick of a child. We are mere ants tripping over one another, hurrying to nowhere.

Even our attempts at worship are tainted. The prophets recognized the danger of religion severed from the source of life. They saw people bringing sacrifices, songs, and gifts to the altar while keeping their hearts tightly closed around personal power and greed, trying to worship without surrendering their hearts for conversion. Jesus recognized the hypocrisy of religion tyrannized by egocentric self-interest. Much of the religion of his day, as it continues to be in ours, was simply an attempt to reduce God to manageable human proportions enabling the devout to preserve the delusion of a relationship with God while guarding their aimless, free-floating greed.

Today, who could argue that many see religion as one more turf to be subjugated to our negotiable terms? A distracted and fretful 40 minutes on a Sunday morning becomes a quick fix for a stressed-out life that we hate while loving it. We fear to turn from the vice-like grip of self-importance and security lest we plunge into the void of our worst fears: to have our delusions of security and privilege taken from us to confront our mortality. Our obsessive self-importance dulls our spirit from the experience of our frightening vulnerability to life's random disregard of our frail self. The dread of our fragile existence awash in a sea of circumstances and events over which we exert only the most fleeting and tentative control is effectively narcotized. This raw material of creative prophetic energy is effectively anesthetized, denied its rightful role in our spiritual quest for true harmony and peace.

Sabbath rest to ponder and wonder at the autonomous wisdom of God unfolding before our eyes through our labor is an imperative engraved in the fiber of the human person. It is a law that rests at the heart of creation just as surely as the rhythms of night and day, winter and summer, waking and resting, the waxing and waning of the moon.

To forget or to neglect the rhythm of life and death, work and rest, word and silence deep within our frames penetrating to the heart of creation is to disrupt and do violence to the sacred, subtle rhythms guiding creation to its end. It is to disconnect ourselves from the current of life that maintains balance, sanity and health in human affairs and our participation in the wisdom of evolution and human history. We become insensitive to our interrelatedness with all beings. Human relationships become adversarial and competitive, serving one's isolated need to survive and prosper even at the expense of others: children, spouse and loved ones, plants and animals. To be still, to withdraw, to become passive becomes unthinkable, a surrender into the seemingly demonic forces threatening to annihilate us.

The cultural insanity so much a part of a capitalistic, consumer society is seen as the birthright of every person. Entering into and becoming a part of the great work frenzy is the dream implanted into every child. We are baptized into church communities that buzz with the frantic energy and symbols of capitalistic success, building religious empires made possible by the efforts of believers who want to share their bounty with a god who, they fondly believe, shares their values and rewards their efforts. Children are educated in schools—church-related schools too—teaching by word and example that success is measured by accomplishments, possessions, and power; that poetic stillness, a silence that seeks to hear the soft whisper of holy wisdom within their hearts, is a waste of time or the domain of the mad and eccentric. At most it should be safely tucked away on a Sunday morning when it cannot interfere with the important things of life. Young children are taught to pray in a way that reinforces and affirms a production-oriented culture priding itself on the quality of its efforts. From earliest childhood we are inducted into a society that owes nothing to anyone, even God. Underlying the American religious tradition is the notion that the blessings we receive from God are the result of our best efforts. This notion has seriously eroded the heart of our prayer and worship, and emptied our spirit of a sense of profound gratitude and humility in the face of the utter gratuity of divine mercy and bounty present in creation. Our modern society has lost sight of the ineradicable, absolute goodness of the human person and the inherent goodness of creation showing forth the wisdom and goodness of the creator. Someone has forgotten to remind us that God cannot *not* love us and therefore no matter what we do or don't do, we are surrounded and enveloped in gratuitous divine love. This notion becomes an affront and insult to the spirit of modern man and woman who cherish their power of making their own way, owing nothing to anyone, even to God. God's bounty and love are seen simply as the well-deserved rewards for a life of effort and striving.

As in all addictions, the return and rewards of our strivings and efforts gradually diminish even as our efforts and exertions increase. The more we do, the less we achieve. The faster and farther we run, the more the horizon recedes, taunting, teasing, mocking, as our efforts become more futile and frantic even while becoming less effective. Finally the addict collapses in rage, defeat and humiliation as despair eats away at the heart. The very heart that has driven us now mocks and shames as the realization dawns that we have chased an illusion. We have been unraveling at the center while being hypnotized by an illusion on the horizon. The illusion so much a part of the Western religious mind-set, particularly evident in the USA today, is the uncritical belief that God is satisfied with religious observance without a corresponding transformation of consciousness and a conversion of behavior and values. In Jesus' view of the reign of God, it is the Samaritan who most clearly understands the role of unqualified love in service to the needy in order to establish God's reign on earth (Lk. 10:29-37). If that is not a clear enough message, Matthew presents the last judgment being determined by the manner in which we cared for the prisoners, the hungry, the naked and the homeless (Mt. 25:31-46).

In the USA today, religious activity and church construction accelerate at a pace rivaled by football and baseball franchises, convenience food restaurants and multi-million dollar athletic stadiums. Alongside this remarkable increase in an interest in religion there is a corresponding increase in crime, a softening of our religious values and the deterioration of our social fabric. The rate of unemployment with its inevitable increase in homelessness is a real threat haunting the lives and security of many who only a few years ago felt safe. Even as the homeless wander in search of a warm and dry or cool place to protect themselves and their families from the elements, we continue to expend religious and public resources on buildings, air-conditioning, carpets or artificial grass for religious and athletic diversions.

Perhaps we are not far from the moment when our denials and evasions will no longer work and we will find waiting for us the gentle, compassionate and healing presence of God ready to receive us into the rest of the Sabbath, where men and women learn once again their true relationship with creation, with themselves, with one another and with God.

Chapter 8

Sabbath:
The Marriage of Time and Eternity

The inability, or unwillingness, to discern the ominous signs of cultural stress with the consequent unraveling of our social fabric characteristic of modern Western capitalistic society is itself an unmistakable symptom of a blindness to our addiction. Denying, minimizing, rationalizations with self-aggrandizing posturing are all indications of our cultural persona peering into the void of our cultural psyche, seeking to convince ourselves that all is well. We celebrate stress, burnout, emotional exhaustion, spiritual apathy as badges of honor bestowed on our cultural heroes who, without question, surrender themselves to the celebration of our shared madness.

At the same time, we callously disengage ourselves from the stark realities of the rampant drug and alcohol addiction, the rapid increase in the incidents of sexual violence perpetrated against children and women, institutionalized assaults against the elderly, the poor and homeless. With appalling self-righteousness, we callously consign men and women who have broken the law to incarceration that shames, humiliates, degrades and breaks the spirit, ultimately suffocating any possibility or desire they might have had to change the course of a life of crime. This is to say nothing of the alarming speed with which our ecosystem erodes around us. Even now the toxic quality of our air and waters is perilously close to life-threatening for many species, as well as the elderly and frail human beings. We prefer to believe that the destruction of the ecosystem is a mere temporary miscalculation which a few minor technical adjustments will remedy, with little or no change in our behavior or patterns of consumption.

In the bedlam of voices promising sure-fire, painless remedies for our social headaches, there runs the quiet, fragile summons of the heart calling to sabbath rest. The simplest, most unassuming and nonviolent solution is the most radical: a conversion of heart and mind that will enable us to turn and face the torrent of madness surrounding us and utter our personal, subtle, but dramatic and life-giving "No;" a "No" to the conventional wisdom that says our true worth is in our accomplishments; a "No" to the lie that says our place in society is measured by the number of the symbols and baubles we have accumulated through our participation in cultural delusions; a "No" to the outrageous childishness that perceives creation and the products of our labor as objects to be mindlessly consumed, toys for our pursuit of selfish gratifications with no heed to the requirements of those with whom we share the earth, or the needs of future generations.

The fundamental question facing each of us is whether or not we can summon the energy to break away from the social and psychological ties that bind us to our cultural identity, to stand apart in the lonely solitude of one who will no longer buy into the conventional wisdom, a wisdom that is in fact a madness.

The healing of the spirit and body that brings the most profound and lasting peace is the quiet and subtle shifts in attitude taking place deep within the self, a surrendering of our hearts to a greater wisdom transcending the rational mind. It comes from truly listening to our pain, opening ourselves to the wisdom buried in the ache of our empty hearts that knows it has been severed from the source of life-giving waters. "As the deer pants for streams of water, so my soul pants for you, O God. My soul thirsts for God, for the living God" (Ps 42:1-2 NJB).

God heard the cry of the people in their slavery (Ex 3:7). Their liberation began under the leadership of a hesitant, shy, and insecure man who knew the bitterness of failure. Moses surrendered his own discouraged heart into the promise of the God of his ancestors, the God who had changed the course of history by purifying the heart of Abraham and Sarah and empowering them with a mystical vision of a new order. From this mystical vision emerged the prophetic boldness enabling them to disengage themselves from the tyranny of Pharaoh and the oppressive temple of their time.

The God of our revelation is a God infallibly known and experienced in liberation and the fullness of life. To truly know God and allow God entrance into our lives is to know the vision of new possibilities; it is to receive the power to break the bonds that imprison our heart. Contrarywise, an equally-infallible sign of the absence of God in human affairs and relationships is the establishment of false gods. We pay allegiance to alien values that demean and imprison, diminish and thwart human potential. The symptoms are inevitable and persistent throughout salvation history, and are unmistakably present in our time. Equally persistent and inevitable is the fidelity of God to the task of calling again and again to the weary hearts of the people to open their hearts and be filled with life-giving waters.

To allow our sickness, our discouragement, our addictions and dependencies to flood our awareness with the reality of our pain is to discover the wisdom that tells us things are out of order, that we have wandered from the law engraved on our hearts, the only allegiance capable of guiding us to authentic peace and true happiness. The suffering of the spirit experienced by so many today reminds us that we have been seduced by false gods promising immediate, if fleeting, gratification. In our suffering and anguish is buried the grace of new possibilities. To find the grace, we need to face the sin.

There is an apparent imponderable paradox in pain. Pain and distress, whether physical or psychic, speak of a deeper reality beneath the surface of our conscious experience. The distress of the Hebrew people sensitized them to the fact that they were not created to be slaves. The pain of their enslaved condition was in itself a sign pointing to their innate longing for self-direction. The fact that they could suffer from their slavery was in itself a sign of psychic health. It was this incessant ache in their hearts that awakened them to the possibility and necessity of freedom and of taking the necessary steps to regain it. Thus, listening to our distress can lead us to the realization of new possibilities. Avoiding pain, narcotizing it, numbs the soul to its hunger for truth. The energy that is meant to be used in creating life is turned inward to live as despair. Despair and cynicism are symptoms of the perversion of our creative energy.

If our pain is excruciating, seeming to drain life's energy, that pain is the threshold of an encounter with our own inner wisdom, the wisdom of God's divine love that created us to live harmoniously with one another and with creation. That harmony is our lost and forgotten inheritance that calls to us from within our anguished hearts. Pain, distress of any kind can be seen as repressed energy available to come forth as dynamic, focused prophetic and creative action.

Our faith journey to God begins with a radical and unambiguous assent to the wisdom and ineradicable goodness of the human person, that divine goodness that extends to the heart of creation. We are called to believe first and foremost, without condition or qualification, in the goodness of the person made in the image and likeness of God. More particularly, we are called to give a radical and heartfelt assent to our particular goodness and embrace our fundamental shared vocation to live under the law that echoes that goodness. It is faith in, and a trusting surrender to that belief, that enables one to grasp the first moment of God's divine self-giving: namely the gift of a body, spirit, mind-self, a self-conscious, self-aware existence in space and time. This self-aware existence is configured to one's body, mind and spirit-self, bearing a name signifying a unique personal existence. It is the totality of this unfolding mystery of a self-aware person, with all its potential for sin and grace, that is opened to a partnership with the Divine. To take possession of the mystery of the self, along with all of the unknown, unimaginable possibilities contained in it, as divine gift is to begin the discovery of the mystery of God's wisdom and the fullness of life unfolding from within the depths of one's being. The fundamental vocation of every person is to become an uncluttered, clear channel through which divine wisdom, truth, and life enter into time and space through human action. This sacramental presence arises from the depths of awareness of our participation in God's creative life. Each human presence and action is a potential sacrament of divine creative action. The fulfillment of the person in time and space is the convergence of divine wisdom with innate human wisdom; human action and divine action converge in the task of continuing the original, primal creative moment when God sent the Word to bring forth truth, beauty, order and harmony from primordial chaos. Abraham, Sarah, Moses and the prophets represent moments in history when hearts and souls were opened to receive the inpouring of the Divine Word and to become true sacraments of God's Wisdom retaking possession of history. In their persons and actions, infinite wisdom and goodness converged and became one with limited human endeavor.

Are we capable of that kind of deep, radical faith today? Perhaps only when all else has failed and the anguish of the social, spiritual pain of our hearts becomes intolerable or undeniable will we find the courage and humility to face the simple, gentle paradox that the solutions to today's problems are as much within us as without. If we can accept the frightening reality that we are, every one of us, as much the cause of our problems as the victims, then we can take the next step towards realizing that, by that fact, we can, each one of us, be the beginning of a healing remedy. If we allow ourselves to attend to the cry of our own hearts and recognize that the cry emerges from a heart disengaged from its true center where the eternal law of God's wisdom is written, we too can become the point of convergence where Divine Wisdom enters our time and place and takes possession of history through our bold action.

It is difficult for our super-rationalized minds to accept what all great teachers, prophets, and religious leaders knew and clearly taught: namely, that each human action, thought and attitude has immeasurable consequences beyond our limited range of perception or imagination. It galls our sense of personal omnipotence and the delusion of our separate self-existence, to be told that our actions, thoughts, values and relationships are not totally subject to our intended purposes and intentions; that, in fact, once released, they have ramifications and consequences far beyond our control. Likewise, to ponder the impact that the lives and decisions of others have had on the quality of our own lives, decisions, and accomplishments grates against an ego that presumes it reigns unchallenged and unopposed over one's sense of supreme individualism. The alienated and inflated ego rages furiously against incursions into its supremacy.

If this truth is disconcerting in its implications, there is a more palatable corresponding aspect to the same reality. For better or for worse, through our seemingly least actions, by the quality of our attitudes, the authenticity of our value system, we are creating our world and our environment. The quality of our life and belief system has an impact on creation and history; the quality of our self-image and sense of purpose and destiny has a telling impact on the lives of others, including the quality of existence experienced by plants, animals and the earth. If we could summon the courage to take a fearless and honest look at the quality of our institutions and our environment and recognize our own souls looking back reproachfully, chiding us, admonishing us to recognize our own sad state, we might take the next humble step toward conversion.

At the heart of our biblical faith is the belief that human life emerges from divine life and reflects divine eternal truth. In union with creation, life unfolds to completion through an amazing and wonderful network of interconnected relationships. In this unfolding evolution of human life we are moving towards perfect union with the divine source of all being. Each one of us is participating in this unfolding drama in our own unique way, giving reality to this mystery in our lives and actions. For better or for worse, each of us is having an impact on creation and history. In this belief we are united to other great religious traditions.

The emphasis of our tradition on sabbath rest is a way of reminding us to stop, to remember our relatedness to the rest of creation, to ponder the mystery unfolding and revealing divine wisdom around us and in us. We are invited to gaze in wonder and awe at this network of interdependence, to be humbled by it, to be reminded of our rightful place within the mystery. This humble and gentle, nonviolent stance can be a radical and disturbing prophetic stance in a society run amok with its egocentric arrogance, placing idolatrous value on isolated human action disassociated from the larger context of the rhythms and cycles of creation, including those running deep within our own body-mind-spirit beings.

In the Book of Exodus (Ex. 23:10-13), we learn that for six years men and women, with their animals and slaves, worked to make the land produce. In the seventh year, those who tilled the soil and watched the flocks surrendered their claim to the fruits of the earth along with their dominion over the land and the fruits of their labor. During this time of sabbatical, they shared the bounty of the earth and the fruits of their labor with the poor, their animals, servants, and slaves. Everyone was cared for by the free bounty of the earth which continued to bear fruit. In a dramatic way bonds between human labor, servants, animals and slaves, as well as the poor, were broken and all stood equally as beneficiaries of the gratuitous riches of our mother the earth. The fruits of one's labor were not a source of power over others, but an occasion for all to celebrate the bounty of the earth and its fruitfulness under human stewardship (Ex 23:10-12). It seems impossible to ponder these biblical imperatives to generosity and humility in the presence of the riches of the earth without being stung by the implicit indictment of our present policies of greed dictating our relationships with our brothers and sisters south of our borders, as well as the poor and unfortunate within our borders. And yet with what appalling arrogance and mindless self-righteousness do we plunder and manipulate the internal political and social affairs of weaker nations to insure that our economic interests are met. Even as we continue our aggressive manipulations of weaker nations, we steadfastly ignore our responsibilities towards the needy in our own land.

As power, control, possessions and the acquisition of personal security have gained ascendency in the human spirit, we have moved further away from a sense of our common dependency on the earth. We are now thoroughly intoxicated with the delusional belief that the true owners of the earth's resources are the ones with the power to extract and manipulate them. As our sense of power increases, our sense of reciprocal give-and-take, of reverence for the needs of earth as a living organism, and of the rightful claims of the poor and needy with whom we share the earth decreases.

We need to find the courage to return to sabbath rest for an hour a day, a half-day or a day a week to contemplate and savor the luxury of knowing that if we are called to work and toil for the completion of creation and the building of the rule of Divine Wisdom, we are also being served and cared for, nourished and caressed by creation. The eternal rhythms of living and dying, the ebbs and flows, rest and action running deep within our hearts are connected to those same rhythmic cycles deep in creation. The living waters running deep within our beings are released from within the tiny, fragile spaces between life and death, rest and action, light and dark, sin and grace. The spirit addicted and in bondage to its own egocentric, heedless pursuits of fleeting gratifications is a stranger to those fragile, still places. To the addicted spirit, even religion becomes one more numbing narcotic, indistinguishable from all the others. Along with football, baseball and the movies, religion takes its place as one more narcotic among many others for the empty spirit of the victims of our rampant consumer society.

To return to sabbath rest as a legitimate and necessary pause within the normal rounds of daily life, to turn inward and lend our inner ear to what is going on in the mind and heart, is to take a stand against the madness that exalts and honors nervous, compulsive egocentricity.

"And he said to them, 'The Sabbath was made for man, not man for the Sabbath; so the Son of man is master even of the Sabbath'" (Mk 2:27-28 NJB). The Sabbath is given to us by Divine Wisdom. It addresses and seeks to call forth and nourish our inner wisdom, enabling us to live sanely and healthfully. Perhaps it is time for us to give heed and recognize our common need for periods of sabbath leisure, creative inaction, to simply be in the presence of one another and creation. Perhaps in that simple presence to one another and our mother the earth, unprotected by our competitive drives, our hunger for affirmation, freed from the compulsion to mindless activity, we might discover the true presence of a living God.

The first, most simple and uncomplicated step on the long path to healing the human family and the earth is the most radical and intimidating—even the most terrifying. That first step takes us into a clear-eyed and frightening encounter with our own collusive participation in the sickness of Western society. To carve out a cave of holy stillness and personal solitude in the midst of the rush of events around us is to apply the most radical remedy to our hearts, one that will awaken us to the absolute imperative of personal conversion. In this personal conversion one returns to true self-possession; it is a step into the freedom of personal responsibility for the quality of life and action that spreads from our own center to create a zone of responsible freedom for others, including the freedom for our earth to freely give of her abundant blessings.

Chapter 9

Contemplation: Detoxifying the Heart

Hopefully our reflections thus far have brought us to an understanding of principles relevant to our circumstances today. The challenge for contemporary men and women is to translate our mythical images into lived responses to current historical realities. All of us have feeling responses towards the unsettling historical realities around us. All too often, we become overwhelmed by the intensity and the enormity of the events and our seeming impotence in the face of reality. Quite understandably, all too many opt for passivity, perhaps even disguising it behind an aura of prayer and resignation to God's will. This feeling of despair, however, is often no more than the breeding ground for cynicism and a self-defeating attitude of helplessness.

Through the contemplative process, our prayerful, patient stillness in the face of the very real pain of our experience of helplessness can be the occasion by which our mythical images shake us loose from self-pity, despair, or cynicism, awakening us to the uncomfortable realization that to accept a reality I know is wrong, to meekly accept helpless passivity, is tantamount to collusion. Allowing our myth to seep into our unconscious is to awaken to our present-day pharaonic oppressors, with their religious and political collaborators, and to discover how they continue to prey on our personal fears and need for security and social approval. Courageous honesty enables one to identify areas of life in which attitudes and values make one vulnerable to participate in the perpetuation of personal unfreedom, thus supporting institutional values and attitudes. Prayer, alive and open to the flow of God's self-revelation in history, responsive to the currents running through the depths of our life, makes us sensitive to God's dynamic presence. We are forced to ask ourselves if we really believe God to be what we say we believe, thus coming face-to-face with the gap between what we say and how we act. We become sensitive to a call to abandon the quest for false security and live in the freedom for which our inner self longs. Prayer sensitizes us, awakens us to the cry of the human spirit around us and in us. The saga and drama of salvation history penetrates our consciousness and becomes active in our life. The adventure of Abraham and Sarah, Moses and the Israelites and all the others right up to our time becomes more than just another story. It becomes our story and we become its continuation through time.

We can draw out specific and identifiable characteristics that mark our understanding of prayer as an opening to, and continuation of, salvation history in our lives.

Our first principle: Prayer is a passive and receptive stance in the presence of God. God's call comes through the lived experience of individual people: you and me. Our prayer opens and sensitizes our hearts to God speaking, acting, creating, redeeming and healing in history. Both Mary's "Behold . . . be it done to me" and Moses' reluctant, stammering assent are models of this quality of prayer. Prayer leads to a spirit that is passive and receptive to God's active, penetrating presence. While it is an awakening to the truth of our suffering condition, it is at the same time a realization of the necessity of responsible choices. When Moses awakened to an awareness of his call, he was also immediately aware of the disconcerting fact that if he didn't act he was, by that fact, a collaborator in the slavery of his people.

A spiritual awakening is at the same time a call to serve because it is an awareness of an emerging freedom coming from within: one's life is no longer one's own. It is the emergence of a deeply felt "No" coming to consciousness, a "No" to the external coercive tyrannies surrounding and suffocating one's spirit. It is the beginning of clear-eyed honesty exposing our personal idols for what they are: tyrants of our own making suffocating the life of our souls and contaminating every aspect of our lives, even our life of worship. Through this humbling encounter with our inner emptiness, with the lies and superficialities that have reigned unquestioned in our lives, we begin the process of opening ourselves to the Divine Wisdom that transforms and purifies our minds and flows into bold creative action. Even in our passive and receptive stance, energy is preparing to flow into concrete, prophetic action. This action begins quietly, oftentimes unnoticed, within our newly-denarcotized hearts. It is the truest meaning of contemplative action: awakening, purifying, humbling, spilling over into prophetic, redemptive presence in the world. Relationships are freed from slavery to the alienated ego, purified and liberated to be more present to persons and material creation in humble service. Unless our prophetic action in the world, our efforts at social or religious reform, our peace-making, our efforts to restore life-generating harmony between ourselves and creation, stem from this inner process of personal conversion and purification, we are simply chasing the shadows of our own puffed-up ego. We are attempting to remake the world, save sinners, tidy up our society, renew the Church to conform to our own self-serving agendas.

Each time one person hears the invitation to grow up and be free to take responsible authority over one's membership in the Church and engagement with the world, the temple and palace lose their suffocating grip on the human spirit. Each time this happens, whether through the conversion of one person, a group, or a church, oppressive structures and conventions are left without their necessary supports to shore up their suffocating oppression of society or persons. The healing of addictive institutions, persons or societies begins by a willingness to step out of the enabler's role.

Our second principle: Prayer heals and restores even as it transforms our understanding and perception of reality. That is to say, prayer is salvific. Abraham and Sarah, Moses and the people of Israel were changed, their consciousness enlarged as they entered into the mystery of their call. New levels of self-awareness were revealed to them. This salvific element of prayer has its internal and external sides. True prayer, grounded on the bedrock of our contemplative tradition, transforms our presence in a given historical epoch from an egocentric presence, mindful only of limited, myopic perceptions, into a courageously-engaged, clear-eyed prophetic presence. The interior purification and transformation brings about renewed relationships and responses to our circumstances. There appears a person or a community of persons, firmly rooted and energized by a vision of what is possible for humanity and what must be done to help bring about the realization of this vision. We discover that our collusive entanglement with oppressive structures, whether political, social, or religious, is symptomatic of our own confused sense of self. As we grow in healthy self-esteem, take appropriate and responsible authority over our lives, the tyranny of external structures lose their hold. Our security becomes firmly rooted in our center where God's Holy Spirit guides and teaches, purifies and enlightens our spirit. The Holy Spirit enlarges our sense of self to an awareness of our innate unity with other persons, plants, animals and the earth. It is in and through this incarnational unity where men and women encounter their most intimate and life-giving union with the living God. Rather than being driven by our alienated ego into service of our own needs and the perceived needs of others, falling deeper into the grasp of our personal ego-image, the Spirit of Jesus enters and calls us to selfless service. Our false, shallow self, the product of conditioning from our parents, our teachers, our society, our economic status, our sectarian religious identity, gives way to our true, core self. Through the dismantling of the idols dominating our sense of self, we give birth to the true self, the self rooted soundly in the life of God, the source of all life, the One who calls all living beings into a unity of peace and harmony. "He is the image of the unseen God, the first-born of all creation, for in him were created all things in heaven and on earth . . . all things were created through him and for him . . . in him all things hold together" (Col 1:15-17 NJB). ". . . God wanted all full-ness to be found in him and through him to reconcile all things to him, everything in heaven and everything on earth, by making peace through his death on the cross" (Col 1:19-20 NJB).

If we are committed to living under the tyranny of our socially conditioned ego, we cannot expect to enjoy the courageous liberty of living in God, and through God, in harmony with creation. All too often today, churches have allowed us to settle for "cheap grace" (Bonhoeffer). The junk food of empty ritual, innocuous academic sermons, mindless adherence to form and routine, scrupulous tidiness in theological thought, abstract norms of ethical behavior, have taken the place of radical conversion of our hearts with the consequent birthing and nourishing of the true self. Thus, while we piously parade to church Sunday after Sunday, our hearts remain hungry and restless. We return to our idols still seeking an elusive solace; our hearts pant for the living God and we have been offered a miniaturized, dehydrated counterfeit.

The price we pay for our efforts to placate the sovereign God, while continuing to protect and defend our adulterous allegiance to cultural and religious idols, is a profound "dis-ease" at the center of our hearts. Prayer and worship built on the solid foundations of our innately contemplative, mystical and prophetic tradition do not allow for cheap compromise or casual convenience. We often forget that the reason sin is an offense to God is because by sin we violate the truth of our humanity. Sinful behavior is a symptom of having forgotten our sacred character, of living as if we had no destiny or purpose greater than the pleasure of the passing moment. Disorder in society and the disintegration of our value system is the result of too many of us living a lie, the lie that says we are our possessions, our accomplishments. We come to believe that we are the person we want others to believe we are. Our true self, the self established in the eternal truth of God, becomes lost and forgotten in the shadows of our unconscious.

In Jesus we glimpse the realization and ultimate fulfillment of God self-revealing in human flesh. Jesus is also the ultimate and definitive revelation of humanity perfectly realized through his life, death and resurrection. He leads the way to the ultimate fulfillment of the Divine Image in each person. Jesus is the image of the totally God-filled human of which Paul speaks in Ephesians (Eph. 3:16-19). Paul is equally bold in assuring us that we have a rightful claim on God's wisdom and truth living in and sharing our human existence, here, now. God's Spirit and our spirits are covenanted in an inner marriage, a marriage that will broach no adulterous dalliances with the spirit of the world. By turning inward, surrounding ourselves in attentive, listening solitude—contemplation—assenting to the truth of the self, we consummate the marriage of our spirit with the Divine Spirit. That same Spirit knows the deep inner mystery of God, the mystery out of which our lives emerge into incarnate reality in time. ". . . to us though, God has given revelation through the Spirit, for the Spirit explores the depths of everything, even the depths of God. After all, is there anyone who knows the qualities of anyone except his own spirit, within him; and in the same way, nobody knows the qualities of God except the Spirit of God. Now, the Spirit we have received is not the spirit of the world but God's own Spirit, so that we may understand the lavish gifts God has given us" (1 Cor. 2: 10-12 NJB). Without this consummation and deepening union our spirits remain empty, restless and vulnerable to the multitude of cultural spirits ready to enter and establish themselves as gods of immediate, if fleeting, gratification. We remain, in spite of our external religious posturing, an empty, "dis-eased" people, sick at heart, spiritually empty. Our sin eats away at our spiritual vitality.

By means of the human spirit open to, and in proper relationship with the Divine, creation is guided to its divinely-appointed end, the reality of which Paul speaks: "For the whole creation is waiting with eagerness for the children of God to be revealed. It was not for its own purposes that creation had frustration imposed on it, but for the purposes of him who imposed it—with the intention that the whole creation itself might be freed from its slavery to corruption and brought into the same glorious freedom as the children of God. We are well aware that the whole creation, until this time, has been groaning in labor pains" (Romans 8:19-22 NJB).

Because our world view has been so erosively influenced by a platonic philosophy positing a fundamental, irreconcilable duality and opposition between matter and spirit, the biblical revelation of a God of harmonious unity, of the integration and reconciliation of all creation, has been lost. Our entire understanding of dynamic divine presence in the creative evolutionary process remains vague at best, or nonexistent in our prayer and worship. We fail to see that Eucharistic love, the love of God incarnate in Jesus, now incarnate in our own flesh and relationships, extends even into our relationship with the earth and the evolutionary process.

The unqualified and uncritical acceptance of Descarte's "I think, therefore I am" has helped disconnect the Western psyche from the intuitive and mysterious currents of our human nature interacting with creation, causing us to denigrate and undervalue the mystical, intuitive, and affective element in our religious heritage. So-called contemplative prayer, life, and worship have been squeezed into tightly-packed boxes of formulas and rituals with scarcely a thought or concern for the fruits of integrated, harmonious living with self and others, much less with creation. Faithful living and radical personal conversion have been tortuously crunched into rigid legalisms measuring human behavior according to abstract principles which rarely, if ever, approximate the lived human experience.

Finally, since the time of Constantine, the Church's quasi-erotic love affair with the political and economic brokers of power and prestige has placed us in a heated, adulterous entanglement with the very power structure we have been called to repudiate and denounce. The secular state has seduced us with the oldest trick in history and effectively neutralized our prophetic voice. A proffered hand of friendship, the promise of a share in the privileges of the power elite, and we were romping in the hay infatuated and enchanted with our civic respectability, intoxicated with the headiness of our share in the power. When we participate—either by silence, word, or action—in this adulterous affair with civic power, we buy into the shameful adultery. We share guilt and responsibility for the oppression, manipulation and humiliation of the victims of our economic and military might. We are a kept people, at the beck and call of the pharaoh and his temple priests, lending the cross to prop up the might of the bomb. This merging and confusion of loyalties is caricaturized in many of our churches by framing altar and sanctuary between papal and American flags. Our marriage covenant with the One God who demands absolute fidelity is reduced to this tragic caricature by rationalizations and emphasis on external religious trivialities, while safely avoiding embarrassing confrontations with the disparities between our daily life and the call to conversion and singleness of heart.

Our third principle emerges from the first and second: Prayer is unifying; it heals and establishes relationships throughout the entire spectrum of our life, even to material creation. Saints like Francis of Assisi exemplify the relationships emanating from union with God. This union of love experienced by Francis poured out in service, not only to persons, but to animals and material creation as well. Prayer draws one from egocentric isolation or ego-serving alliances into proper and true relationships. In prayer we "re-member" who we are in relation to God, other persons, creation. Within the flow of history we open our minds and hearts to the realization of our commonly-held vision contained in our biblical myths. Prayer reconnects us at a most fundamental level of human existence and religious belief. By "re-membering" we put the broken, disconnected and forgotten pieces of our existence back where they belong, in our heart-center where God's redemptive presence and ours meet and become one. In the heart-center, all divisions, separations, brokenness are melted and transformed by Divine love pouring into and being configured to our true humanity, created in the divine image. Contrary to the conventional lie of our time, the natural state of the human person is loving communion with other persons, animals and plants. When we are released from the tyranny of our stingy self-absorption, we encounter the living God. Liturgy, ethics, law, pious devotions and creeds can never substitute for this radical conversion. Through this conversion we are awakened to the realization of our capacity for love.

In the language of Hebrews 4:12-13, we surrender ourselves to the Word that cuts, opens, reveals, and probes our innermost secret thoughts. The heart that is hardened by defensiveness, fear, the need to control and make things work according to plan is a heart impermeable to the creative action of God's redemptive Word; it is a heart closed in and surrounded by its self-imposed boundaries. This person's Scripture reading, devotions and pious practices emanate from a wishful desire to believe that God is saying what one wants to hear, reinforcing personal fantasies and desires. When the Word of God can get no farther than the analytical and rational, then the mystery of the Word is subject to limited, culturally-conditioned presuppositions. Brain power, disengaged from the wisdom of the body, the emotions and intuition, the language of the heart-center, subjects God's Word of infinite mystery to the boundaries of impoverished human intelligence and egocentric self-interest.

If I have a need for authority, prestige, control, I can find ample reinforcement in the Bible to assure me that God is behind my efforts. We interpret God's Word rather than allow ourselves and our actions to be interpreted and judged by it, enlarging the horizons of self-awareness.

The intense drive for power, prestige, and control is reinforced by a conviction that God is one of us, sharing our values and supporting our individual or national grasping for dominance of Third World economies and political systems. The world has yet to hear even a hint of an apology for the holocaust of tens of thousands of innocents at Nagasaki and Hiroshima. We arrogantly perpetrated unspeakable obscenities in southeast Asia, more recently in Central and South America. The significance of the slaying of the six Jesuits and two women in El Salvador is increased, and the outrage intensified for North Americans, by the fact that five of the nine soldiers involved were trained by the American military at taxpayer expense at the School of the Americas in Ft. Bening, GA. The people of El Salvador pay heavily for our uncritical readiness to believe in the righteousness of our foreign policy. In this latest conflict, in the Middle East Americans on every level asked our youth to risk their lives for the preservation of our gas-guzzling, petroleum-addicted behavior. It is this arrogant appropriation of divine righteousness than enables Americans and other First World nations to disregard, deny or minimize the incalculable suffering and destruction brought on by our unprecedented use of high technology and primitive fire power to assert our will in the Middle East. This high-handed disregard for human life and the enthronement of raw power speaks eloquently of a nation that has lost its soul. As long as we continue to be steeped in the delusion that God is somehow a willing partner in our adventurism, our errors will continue as our claim to moral leadership diminishes.

Parents, teachers, pastors, lovers, politicians, popes and theologians pull down divine authority to substantiate and reinforce their manipulative use of power to serve their purposes. There is no more fierce opponent on earth than one who believes that God is on his or her side. "God wills it!" enabled crusading Christians to massacre unbelievers by the tens of thousands. In one form or another that belief has energized invading armies, fueled inquisitions, tortured dissidents, and fueled the pens of church authorities as they wrote condemnations and interdicts against those with the temerity to challenge their unilateral authority to define and promulgate their interpretation of divine truth. The actions that murdered the prophets and crucified Jesus were fueled by the same energy, the dark sinister energy that had invaded, and continues to invade, religious and political authorities, tyrannized by their inflated ego, infuriated and enraged by assaults on their sovereignty.

That same dark energy continues to invade the hearts of those who seek the security of having someone take responsibility for how they act and what they believe. If churches and political systems are able to dominate, oppress and control, it is because there are many with the need to believe what they are told, to abdicate their inner authority to others. Recently the U.S. was able to mount and sustain an unprecedented military action in the Middle East by manipulating citizens only too ready to believe that their political leaders are anointed with divine wisdom. The prophetic voices of church leaders during this time were tragically ambivalent. A truly authentic church community informs and frees the conscience to critique public policy, whether those policies be of church or state. When religion and church are alive by being connected to the heart-center of men and women, the bondage of mindless political and religious loyalties are broken or at least diluted.

Finally, a fourth principle: Prayer is liberating and enlarging. Prayer liberates and enlarges the heart as it reveals the tyranny of our idols. It energizes us to prophetic action in the face of attitudes, values and traditions that hold the hearts of men and women in bondage. The prophets, reformers and religious guides of contemplative traditions operated out of a deep-seated conviction that persons were called to freedom. The early Christians considered personal liberty from external authority synonymous with Gospel. Gospel was freedom from external coercion, whether from temple authorities, political rulers or social conventions. The inner freedom of the spirit was a sure sign of the presence of the Holy Spirit. This appropriation of personal authority was grounded in a conviction of the innate nobility and goodness of human nature. True nobility and virtue could only emerge and flourish in a community of people who knew interior freedom.

Martin Luther King, Dorothy Day, and many others serve as modern-day examples. Freedom escapes from our heart like an aroma when the seal is broken. It is not something we do, but rather it is the inevitable result of the natural inclination towards truth and goodness for which we have been created. Our life inclines towards freedom and truth, just as the plants incline toward the light. Freedom and holiness are synonymous; holiness (love) is not something we make happen. It is the natural and proper state of our humanity to which our heart naturally inclines. Holiness is the thrust towards Divine truth revealed within fleshed humanity. Holiness happens, freedom comes, wisdom blossoms when the heart awakens to the reality and pain of its slavery and allows the truth to unfold, guided by the uncompromising light of God's Word. We are led to that state of perfect unity and light for which we have been created.

On the other hand, the heart inoculated against pain is insensitive and unaware of its natural longing and search for the infinite. One accepts slavery to the status quo as the inevitable human condition, never questioning, never challenging or critiquing the arbitrary bondage to conventional religious, social and political mediocrity. The ultimate capitulation to the power of slavery is to convince ourselves that it is God's will and bind ourselves in obedience to accept it as our rightful place. In the twisted logic of our cultural ego, ignorance and slavery become a virtue.

Another subtle and devious trick of the inflated ego is to project fantasies of holiness and goodness onto others: popes, priests, nuns and saints, heroes and heroines. Thus, the soul is numbed to the possibility that it is oneself who is called to be the saint. Through this subterfuge of false humility, the ego purrs away contented and undisturbed, secure in its continued delusion of well-being.

As light enters our darkness, one becomes free to withdraw projections of holiness and goodness onto heroes and heroines. We realize that those whom we had previously considered saints or heroes are not much different from us. They are seen as people seeking to do what they honestly know how to do, not being held back by their real or imagined shortcomings. We understand that the major difference between St. Francis or St. Ignatius and ourselves is the courage with which they embraced their responsibility to act. As saints and heroes outside of oneself diminish in their stature, one's own sense of responsibility enlarges. The saint and sinner are no longer seen to be other persons, but realities living side by side within oneself. I am the saint as well as the sinner. One is faced with the startling realization that if there are to be saints, prophets, mystics in the world, they wait to be born from within our impoverished, barren souls. Our inner life becomes the place where new life blossoms forth, life-giving waters flow.

As this process takes place and one becomes more "self-possessed," the only legitimate author of one's story, there is less need to possess others, to cling to the hope and expectation that happiness and well-being will be satisfied by the actions and accomplishments of others. One is at peace with the saint as well as the sinner one knows oneself to be. Grounded in the firm conviction of one's innate goodness and truth, realizing that one possesses the necessary raw material to create life, others are allowed to be who they are. Personal affirmation and inner freedom free others. Our personal presence becomes a zone of freedom allowing others to taste their own freedom. Just as negative thinking tends to spill over and contaminate the psychic environment, so too is freedom and an enlightened consciousness contagious. The dream and the challenge of communities grounded in this reality begin in the heart of each person who, like Abraham and Sarah, Moses and the Israelites, Mary and the Apostles, turns even for a moment to hear the inner restlessness, and in that restlessness discerns the Word of God addressing us today. "If only you would listen to God today; do not harden your hearts." (Heb. 4:7).

A praying community is a community grounded on the unshakable conviction and commitment to the mandate to radical freedom to grow and become in the authenticity of one's God-given uniqueness. Only when church is grounded in this conviction and commitment can it be true and life-giving. The obedience of Jesus to Divine Wisdom was founded on a sure knowledge and commitment to his divinely-authored human nature and the possibilities contained in it. Rooted in this truth, he walked among men and women, awakening in them a realization and acceptance of their truth and goodness. He helped them "re-member" who they were. Jesus' fleshed humanity was God's sacrament of liberty. We are called to nothing less. Our shared vocation is to be the body of Christ in history. This is the bedrock upon which Christian community, Church, is founded. Neither obedience nor Church, much less obedience to Church, can exist without this personal grounding in a commitment to our own God-authored human promise, hidden, often-times forgotten, but nonetheless real. Our ineradicable goodness, our participation in divine goodness and wisdom is the treasure for which we must sell everything else (Mt. 13:44). It is the determination to possess this treasure that fuels our obedience, provides the energy to leave everything else as we single-mindedly set ourselves about the task.

Without this grounding, obedience becomes one more tool of institutional manipulation and coercion, blessed by domesticated and docile institutional gods created to serve institutional needs. Obedience and community, instead of being life-giving pillars of Church, grounded deeply in a shared relationship with God, become prisons limiting and diminishing the growth of God's image in our souls and divine freedom in our actions. Our prayer, nourished in the waters of our contemplative, mystical and prophetic tradition, leads us to become the contemplative, mystic and prophetic presence capable of redeeming and transforming our portion of history. The conversion of our church into a truly listening community, gathering in worship to attend God's Word, being grasped by the vision of the divine promise fulfilled in our time, energetically engaging our world with the boldness of the prophet, happens one person at a time, one community at a time.

"*. . . if today you hear God's voice, harden not your hearts.*"

Chapter 10

Remembering:
Renewing the Vision

I have attempted to demonstrate that the contemplative-mystical-prophetic element of our prayer and worship are more than abstract, academic theories taking place chiefly in the mind. Nor can they be described as specifically willed acts formulated in the mind and executed in deliberate patterns of behavior. In fact, these are qualitative experiences of power, contributing substantively to our every and least action. Contemplative-mystic-prophetic qualities are the marks of a personality transformed as the result of a personal conversion. A new set of values becomes operative, freeing us from unconscious bondage to unredeemed conventional values. Contrary to popular belief these qualities are inherent in our tradition and, under proper circumstances, will be the normal fruit of authentic prayer. In other words, authentic prayer nourishes normal human growth and development into mature, responsible, and healthy adult living.

This entire process can be understood within the context of remembering. Throughout our biblical myth there is a constant effort to remember the events and people that form the core of the community's identity. The people know who they are in the present because of the events making up their past, enabling them to believe in and hope for future, if still unknown, possibilities. From their present, they faced the future rooted in a core identity connecting them to a living tradition. They lived with confidence in its continued deepening into the future. For our Jewish Mothers and Fathers in the faith, their rituals and feasts kept alive the great historical events and persons that formed the substance of their communal identity. They understood these events as living and operative in their immediate lives and decisions. The Exodus, the Sinai experience, the sojourn in the wilderness were experiences carved into the souls of individuals, bonding them into a community of people distinct and unique among other peoples. This current of life passed from one generation to another. To celebrate Passover was to plumb the depths of their identity, to discover the story of their present lives connecting with the larger stream of Jewish history. Memory was the entranceway through which their lives, perhaps generations removed from the original events, encountered and became one with the great epochs of their history.

As historical circumstances changed from generation to generation, their living memory of the key events enabled them to translate them into contemporary expression relevant to their understanding of their experience. As new challenges and crises arose, their core identity served as a pool of wisdom and dynamic inspiration from which they created their response to the present and faced into their future. History was the sacrament of their relationship with God; this relationship was bonded by maintaining intact their connectedness to their history. Events in that history were the hammer and anvil upon which their knowledge and service of God was formed.

When Christ celebrated Passover with his friends, he invited them to remember with him the pivotal event of their shared history, to remember in ritual the mighty power of God working in the lives of their ancestors, and which they hoped would deliver them from their present oppression. Throughout this meal they were led to remember that this astonishing manifestation of divine power was to be received into their lives, made dynamically present in faith and action, and passed on to future generations. Unsuspectingly they were being led into an awesome and unforgettable new revelation that probed the memory deeper, laying it open to a new revelation until now hidden within the original event.

Just as the original passing over became the core memory of the Jewish people, so too would the passing-over of Jesus become the center around which the early Christians would attempt to understand and weave their identity. The memory of Jesus, the events of his life, were now to become the foundations around which the Christian community would forge and articulate a new and dramatic way of being present in the world and facing into history.

The first generation of Christians was a community of persons who had shared an extraordinarily disturbing and perplexing experience, one that had shattered their previous ways of believing and understanding their religious heritage. It radically altered their way of responding to and interacting with the world in which they lived. In some way, this experience of Jesus—who died, but was again present in their midst with a new power—punched through to their core experience of being human, opened them to new ways of addressing the fundamental questions of human life and the struggle for meaning.

The Acts of the Apostles clearly indicate that a power was released where, before, there had been fear, boldness where there had been timidity; freedom where there had been oppression of all kinds: religious, socioeconomic, political. They were facing life with power, a power that drove out fear, erased self-interest, and freed them from false loyalties (Acts 2:1-13;42-47;7). Keeping it alive and dynamic in the everyday lives and actions of the first communities was the sole objective of their liturgical gatherings and the celebrations of the great events in the life of the young Church. The emphasis was on the transmission and deepening understanding of the great power that had been released upon the world and of which they were the recipients and designated transmitters. In this experience of the first generations of Christians we see the elements of the contemplative, mystic and prophetic drawn into one intense outpouring of creative energy, confronting the status quo even as it proclaimed the arrival of the new.

The key concepts here are power and energy translated into bold and prophetic presence, courageous action and selfless service. Important to remember is that this power for prophetic and fearless living was transmitted and actualized in lived experience. The community of believers was the depository of the power of Christ, and through the community, individuals were empowered to live in and for Christ. The believing community was a zone of freedom empowering people to step beyond conventional values and cultural roles—religious as well as secular—and "put on Christ." The new person in Christ was a person unconditionally affirmed in his or her personal truth and validated in their uniqueness. Their presence repudiated conventional norms of behavior and thinking, making them a source of irritation and bewilderment to their contemporaries. Belief in the resurrection took away the sting and therefore the tyranny of the fear of death. The boundaries of life had been expanded beyond death to eternal life. Now the future opened up, not only through time, but into eternity.

We are touching here on the healing power of the shared memory of a real person who lived, suffered, died and was now mysteriously present in their lives. This memory of a shared experience brought about integration and wholeness from previously fragmented and disconnected remnants, random events with few if any cohesive links. What had previously been experienced as powerlessness and the need for personal safety and security, the acquisition of personal power, was now given a wholeness that completely changed their way of perceiving and responding to life. Individual lives and experiences were intersected by a larger reality and drawn into fuller meaning. Life with all its mystery transcended the narrow limits of a terrifying and deadening personal isolation. Sinners, gentiles, the foreigners, the sick and forgotten were now equal, the valid recipients of love and compassionate understanding with unqualified acceptance into a community. The community was beginning to understand itself as members of one living body, the body of Christ. The Body of Christ was not a mere abstraction but the realization that, gathered in community bound by the teaching of the Apostles, they were the living flesh into which the very life of God flowed and passed into historical presence. The power of the Holy Spirit penetrated and possessed their heart. Theology emerged out of, reflected on, and sought to articulate the prior experience. As reflection on the meaning of the experience developed through the generations, so too did the theology. But theology always reflected on and sought to serve the unfolding experience, never to substitute for it.

Memory is essential for healthy living. To lose contact with the past is to be set adrift in an ocean of terrifying meaninglessness. Without rootedness in the past, there is no context in the present from which to form a sense of "I," a continuous core self that moves through personal history. Without memory the future looms as a terrifying repetition of the present aimlessness. This is as true for groups as it is for individuals.

Psychoanalysis and other forms of therapy often aim at digging out long-forgotten pains and reintegrating them, "re-membering," to give them their rightful, if painful, place in our history. Our life is not complete, cannot be fully savored so long as our personal or shared history is dismembered, selectively anesthetized. The Hebrew people remembered and celebrated their infidelities, therein recognizing the merciful tenderness of a God who never abandoned them. The apostles and disciples remembered and wondered at their own stubborn lack of understanding, marveling at their failure and timidity, thereby highlighting the compassionate mercy of the Savior. Our true appreciation and full participation in the saving mystery depends as much on remembering and accepting our sinfulness as our virtues.

Religion is the traditional carrier of group memories, enabling succeeding generations to build meaning into their life's struggles and to provide a ground from which the future can be faced and engaged with hope. Through ritual, customs, and shared beliefs about the purpose of life people receive support in their struggles, strength in the knowledge of forgiveness and the possibility of reconciliation and healing. Life is lifted out of the narrowness of isolated existence and drawn into a larger meaningful context.

The Word that became incarnate in Jesus is the Word that comes to uncover and address the human longing for meaning and purpose, our need for the assurance that we are forgiven and reconciled, that our failures and sins fit into a larger perspective. We become the meeting place between the world and God's promise of redemption. In prayer, one allows the redemptive Word to penetrate and probe, reveal and know the deep heart, wherein lies our own untold story of forgotten and repressed dreams and pains. Unrealized and unrecognized longings and fears, shameful sins and terrifying weaknesses wait to be called forth and recognized as true and equal participants in the creation of one's life. Memory, individual and group, is the current into which the Word is received, made healing and redemptive in the lived experience of persons in a community of prayer and faith, and transmitted as a living experience from generation to generation.

Now we will attempt to place the contemplative, mystical and prophetic qualities of prayer on their own foundation, or three essential pillars, all of which must be present if our prayer is to be integrating and healing. These three essential pillars are eminently and logically grounded in our myth.

These essential ingredients of prayer provide the earthy reality enanbling us to become the centered and integrated persons wherein spirit and matter, sin and grace, light and darkness, heaven and earth, are drawn into a creative and life-giving union. They are: 1) attentive listening to our body- mind-spirit self; personal re-membering as participation in salvation history, 2) attention to the present historical circumstance; that is, attending to the historical process out of which the present rises, and 3) attention to God's continuing self-revelation in a community of faith, tradition, and Sacred Scripture; remembering and making present and active the salvation myth.

By means of these qualities present in our prayer, we translate the salvation myth into relevant action addressing contemporary circumstances. Contemplation can now be seen as a way of opening and sensitizing ourselves to the living memory of God's redemptive act continuing in history, but more importantly, continuing in the individual life of every person in the believing community. It sensitizes us to recognize the present as the arena in which these saving acts continue. Our life is seen as a participation in the common condition of humanity, in need of continuing healing.

The first moment of God's self-revelation to us is our mind-body-spirit existence endowed with a capacity for self-awareness in relationships. Our body-self is an essential participant in this network of relationships. To ignore or minimize the role of the body with its vast array of feelings and sensations is to deprive ourselves of an extraordinary means of perception and knowledge. Indeed, the body has its own wisdom which complements the wisdom of the mind. A reverent and prayerful attention to the body can be the means of a rich and fruitful participation in life unavailable through intellectual and rational faculties alone. Body-prayer leads to an awareness and sensitivity to the various inner movements calling attention to signs of weariness, early subtle indications of approaching sickness, the need for more rest or quiet time. Often, it is the body where the first faint signs of the emergence of new self-understanding, or the need to make adjustments in one's external life is sensed. The body, if attended to and given its rightful place in one's conscious life, can be a powerful ally in developing a healthy and satsifying life in harmony with one's inner truth.

Through a positive relationship with the body and a disciplined effort to become sensitive to it as a source of wisdom, one begins the process of entering into a deeper and richer relationship with the entire spectrum of intuition, feelings, physical sensations and emotions. Once drawn into conscious participation in life, the body is capable of leading us to new depths of self-understanding. Prayer, rather than being restricted to the intellect and will, becomes multi-dimensional, leading to a dialogue with material creation and heretofore unrealized sources of energy.

The first moment of prayer is marked by awareness of the experience of life as it flows into and through one's particular corporal existence. One understands and accepts the tremendous reality that life, in all its various dimensions, is an ongoing word of Divine revelation. One's very existence is recognized and accepted for the sacred event that it is: a sacrament of God's saving acts. The body is the means of bringing thought, dreams, wishes and urges into concrete action. To be in daily, disciplined dialogue with our body-self is to open the way to healthy, spontaneous and creative interaction with all dimensions of life. This principle is affirmed by recalling that the major mystical traditions of the world, without exception, incorporate well defined bodily disciplines and physical postures to ensure the body's full participation in our pursuit of divine union. It is a quite recent development in the western world that has tended to minimize the role of the body in the spiritual life while emphasizing the role of the intellect and will.

The second pillar on which prayer is established is a heart attentive to the ebb and flow of history going on in and around us. "The signs of the times" are constantly ringing in our ears, pounding on the door of our inner self, our heart, reminding us of our membership and participation in an enterprise that began long before us, extends beyond our own frail center, and into the far horizons of future history. If we believe that God creates and guides history, then we must believe that we are the sacraments of a new possibility for the historical process. Men and women, in the daily toil of living, are co-creators nurturing and guiding creation to completion. Each one of us is the promise of a new beginning, a fresh alternative, a new creation modeled on the Christ, the Word sent to remind us of who we are and what our lives are all about.

Modern Christians welcome the Christ event into their lives and into history. We rejoice with Mary who was not unaware of the plight of her people under the domination of a foreign power. "My soul proclaims the greatness of the Lord and my spirit rejoices in God my savior; because he has looked upon the humiliation of his servant" (Lk. 1:46-47 NJB). We, in communion with the patriarchs, prophets, Mary and the apostles, believe that the promise made by God to his people can be, will be, fulfilled in us. With a sound and holy belief in our self as God's handiwork, called to be sacraments of the living Word, we believe, with Mary, that God can do mighty things in and through us. Prayer will lead us to that fragile point where the cry of our own heart meets and blends with the cry of the heart of the human family and the earth. Prayer enables us to maintain an attentiveness to the action and reaction of the currents of life in and around us. To cut ourselves off from one or the other is to distort and impoverish our participation in life. Just as we believe that the individual person is the point of encounter between God and History, we also believe that the larger contemporary historical scene reveals Divine action and contains the promise of divine creative power. To the believing person, the Divine presence is known and served even in the darkness and chaos of wars and violence, suffering and injustice. The faithful person listens and attends to God's self-revelation in history. Pain, suffering, injustice, violence, while disheartening, become occasions for faithful prophetic action.

The third pillar supporting our contemplative listening is God's living Word in Sacred Scripture and the ongoing presence of the Holy Spirit in a community of faithful people. Sacred Scripture is one aspect of God's eternal Word, spoken from all eternity, and eternally bringing about the reality it speaks. Thus, there is a special relationship between our heart-center and God's Word received, reflected on and shared through a community of faith. Our hearts have been created specifically to attend to and receive the Word, to give it flesh as Mary did, as the Prophets and the body of the faithful have throughout the centuries. Our heart will not know life, peace and rest until it is encountered by God's Word spoken in Jesus Christ remembered and given presence in a community of praying persons. The other side of that formula is that God's Word needs the flesh of our hearts in order to come to completion and fruition in time.

The greatest obstacle to hearing and receiving the Word of God is within our hearts. We cannot entertain the desires of our alienated egos and the Word of God at the same time. The parable of the seed in Matthew becomes strikingly pertinent for our reflections. He said,

> "Listen, a sower went out to sow. As he sowed, some seeds fell on the edge of the path, and the birds came and ate them up. Others fell on patches of rock where they found little soil and sprang up at once, because there was no depth of earth; but as soon as the sun came up they were scorched and, not having any roots, they withered away. Others fell among thorns, and the thorns grew up and choked them. Others fell on rich soil and produced their crop, some a hundred-fold, some sixty, some thirty. Anyone who has ears should listen." (Mt.13:4-9 NJB).

The rich soil is a contemplative heart firmly established on the three pillars of a reverential attention to God's Wisdom unfolding from within the body-mind-spirit self, the contemporary historical situation, and Sacred Scripture reflected on and lived in history. Through the contemplative process, the Church becomes a gathering of people with hearts receptive to the Word of God speaking through creation and history. Into that contemplative heart, open, sensitive and fertile, penetrates the Word of God to bring forth a rich harvest of new possibilities for humanity and humanity's mother, the earth. By reawakening the contemplative, mystic and prophetic elements of our faith, a person, a community, a church is transformed into a fertile womb of new life for the world.

The public ritual of the Church is essentially a public rite of collective contemplation in which we "re-member" and make present in our lives the event of Christ's resurrection breaking into the lives of the apostles and disciples. We join our lives to the acts of adoration, praise and sacrifice of our Mothers and Fathers in the faith who have handed on the collective memory to us. In our lives that event remains alive and active. When we join our prayer to the prayer of the community the Christ event of history intersects and joins with the mystery of our life. The Christ event is particularized in our life; our life is universalized through the Christ event living and acting in us. In our public prayer and service, the saints, confessors, martyrs, and sinners, are drawn into and given presence in our collective gathering. Their fidelity in trial, failure, persecution and prophetic action bears fruit in our gathering, connects us to the past and opens us in union with them, to the future. By our connectedness to their lives and actions in faith, their work is drawn to a new level of completion through ours, just as ours will be left incomplete to be finished by future generations.

As we doggedly discern our immediate task in life, the truly praying community is drawn into the larger, global life of the human family. We find ourselves one in our hearts as we join in the struggle for justice with Vietnamese, Tibetan, Chinese Buddhists and Daoists, Hindus, Mohammedans, South African Blacks, Central American Base Communities, Native Americans and Afro-Americans and Christian feminists. Our hearts are opened to the universal human quest for meaning and peace. We lend our prayer and the power of our voice and prophetic action to the sufferers of the world whose heart continues to cry out to the One God. In our hearts, the cry of the people continues to ascend to God. We, like Moses, are called and sent to undo the religious, social, and political oppressors of our day.

Chapter 11

Awakening:
Dying Into Life

The problem of an uncritical acceptance of our social, cultural, and religious environment is an important point needing serious reflection when considering the issue of prayer and evangelical living. The Gospel demands that we choose between the cross, putting on the mind and heart of Christ, or settling for compromise, accommodation to the unredeemed values of an unenlightened humanity. To avoid the painful necessity of making clear choices between gospel values and the values of society is, in the long run, to participate in and support values and structures that dehumanize and demean the spirit of modern men and women, ultimately allowing society to slip further and further away from the guidance of Divine Wisdom.

Our biblical tradition seeks to bore through our limited self-consciousness, determined by immediate cultural perceptions, to remind us that ultimately we are connected to one another and to creation through our common origins in a Divine creative act. Furthermore, we are bonded together by our common sharing of the earth with its life-sustaining resources, especially our shared dependency on the quality of the air we breathe and the water we drink.

The goal of our effort to live an evangelical life is to grow into Christ-consciousness; a sense of self, fully aware of the unity of all being in the life of the creator. This is a concrete, tangible reality bearing fruit in action and transformed behavior. It is the fruit of conversion and a renewed heart. The tribal and personal ego is to be purified from the tyranny of personal and cultural narrowness and freed to participate in the unity and interdependence of all beings on earth.

Christian community, sacrament, liturgy and personal prayer are all commonly aimed at bringing about this transformation and awakening to this reality. Running throughout Judeo-Christian tradition is the belief that creation, seen and unseen, is the result of a divine creative act. "In the beginning was the Word: the Word was with God and the Word was God. He was with God in the beginning. Through him all things came into being, not one thing came into being except through him. What has come into being in him was life . . ." (Jn 1:1-4 NJB). Man and woman are the epitome of this creative act, and who, with creation, are bound in this common origin and the sustaining power of the creator. It is only within the network of this interdependence that we fully know and grasp the meaning of existence. Until we are redeemed from the illusion of separations and divisions that dominate our perceptions and motivate our actions, we will not understand the meaning of life.

By the time most of us have reached young adulthood, we are thoroughly encased in a tightly-knit web of perceptions, values, biases, cultural and religious assumptions from which we establish our personal identity within our cultural group. The horizons of our self-awareness have reached beyond immediate family to include friends, religious affiliation, socioeconomic and political identity to the outer limits of our national and racial boundaries. By the very fact of this identification, we also exclude and separate ourselves from the majority of other people inhabiting the earth.

The groups with which we identify in turn count on us to support them and expend our lives and energies contributing to their survival through history. We are expected to make sacrifices, even die or kill others in the defense of our group and all that it stands for. At stake is our sense of self. What we call loyalty is generally motivated by our egocentric desire to preserve the institutions and values that provide us with an identity and sense of belonging. Thus our ego boundaries are first established in tribal loyalties and the institutions of the family like church, ethnic heritage, political affiliation, socioeconomic status and the like. These institutions provide a stability of place and time that serve as reference points telling us, and others, who we are and what we stand for. From there our ego boundaries extend out to national and more general common interests. Always, however, this membership identity is grounded in an acutely felt need for personal survival. Personal security and survival are intimately connected with the well-being and survival of our group. Our experience of personal immortality consists in a sense of historical continuity, the perpetuation of our name and lineage, as well as all of the supporting institutions and values through history and into the future.

The truly innovative pioneer of the journey to consciousness is such only because he or she becomes aware of what is possible beyond the frontiers of tribal, national, or ethnic identity, and moves toward the realization of a self-awareness embodying other persons and creation. Such a person naturally brushes against frontiers and parameters established to stabilize and focus our loyalties. Conflict arises when resistance to the unknown, the unpredictable is encountered. An egocentric attachment to the comfort and security of the status quo is oftentimes seen as loyalty. Innovators, inspired by dreams of what is possible, are oftentimes seen as subversive to the sacred status quo. Resistance to change is engendered from our own inner resistance to leaving what we know and trust in order to venture into the risk of the unknown. Often we simply do not sufficiently trust ourselves to embark on our own journey of self-discovery. This is in large part due to the fact that our culture in general, parents and surrogate parental institutions like church, school, political party, etc., do not encourage creative innovation. This entrapment in security and conformity to tribal values is as often as not institutionalized in uncritical acceptance and defense of our socioeconomic, religious and political affiliations. We in turn "demonize" our enemies by seeing them as threats to all that we consider to be good, holy and true. We sacralize our limited cultural perceptions by identifying them with God's will, divine revelation, and other such terms, which add an element of mystery we fear to tamper with. In this way we learn to uncritically accept decisions of authority, traditions and customs handed down with the aura of unquestioned divine mandate. When this happens we are ripe for the "holy war" against evil, evil being anyone who calls into question our preferred way of looking at the world or our understanding of God. It is rare that a nation undertakes any kind of war or foreign adventure without first being convinced that it is "God's will" and the cause just. Slavery continued in the United States for as long as it did because good people had been convinced, and passed that belief from generation to generation, that slavery was God's plan for the black people. The "superior" white race believed it was fulfilling a divine mandate in seeing to it that the slaves were kept in their divinely-ordered place. For generations South Africa maintained strict racial segregation because of similar religious convictions. As individuals, black as well as white, awakened to the inhumanity of the institution of slavery, they were identified as subversive at least, and at most as destroyers of a divinely-ordered plan for society.

To grasp the meaning of our salvation myth is to see and understand our common call to confront priest and pharaoh as did Abraham and Sarah, Moses and the Israelites in the Hebrew Testament, as did Christ and his followers in the Christian covenant. The community of Acts most eloquently dramatizes this movement away from conventional beliefs and behavior during the post-Resurrection Church and extending into the first several centuries of Christian history. Because their minds had been opened to entertain new possibilities, they repudiated the previous religious and political conventions that had held minds and imaginations in bondage. They were therefore seen as enemies of the state and religion, heretics worthy of imprisonment, exile and death.

When the consciousness of Moses was awakened to the possibility of alternatives for himself and his people, he encountered resistance from the pharaoh as well as from those within the ranks of the Israelites who would rather have made accommodations to their situation. For some Israelites, the security and sense of well-being far outweighed the demeaning humiliation of their slavery. The pharaoh's military and economic power depended on keeping the Israelites in line. Those Israelites who chose comfort and security over the risk of new possibilities and alternatives formed an alliance of mutual self-interest with their own oppressors.

When Martin Luther King picked up the challenge afforded by Rosa Parks, he had to encounter resistance not only from the white establishment, but elements within the black establishment as well. They failed to understand the vision of freedom and new possibilities for all people, blacks as well as whites. Over the years they had accommodated themselves to the system of segregation, had found a modicum of comfort and security and saw little or no reason to risk losing these dubious gains. Underneath this resistance we can discern in the black community a lack of basic trust and belief in their own right to be free. Just as the Israelites before us, today our defense of the institutions that enslave us betrays the insidious manner in which we take on the identity provided by our present day pharaohs. We believe about ourselves what they want us to believe. We become the defenders and supporters of our own political and religious slavery.

When Christ came on the scene and sought to awaken people to their immediate relationship to a God who desired the fullness of life and freedom for creation, this immediately threatened the sense of well-being and identity of those who had become safe and secure in their religious authority over others. It also challenged those who found comfort in the safety and security of salvation through rubric, ritual and law. For those who had abdicated authority over their lives to the security of temple law and religious ritual, the prospect of personal responsibility and freedom to make choices, and be responsible for those choices, appeared foolhardy and arrogant. In the eyes of the religiously secure who derive comfort and security from having someone else tell them what is right and wrong, Jesus would appear as subversive to the public ecclesial or political order.

Moses and Jesus were not revolutionaries in the political sense of the word. They were most certainly and unambiguously innovative pioneers of the human spirit and the hidden potential living within the folds of our inner life. They awakened people to new depths of human possibility and therefore brushed against the established parameters of the social structures. Most certainly, the religious structure charged with mediating and monitoring the relationship of men and women with God would feel threatened by the notion of an immediate access to God through the human heart. This radical notion calls and continues to call hallowed religious tradition into question, along with the careers and identities of all those entrusted with religious authority. The two forces most unambiguously and brutally opposed to Jesus and to Moses were the two which had the most to lose from their message: the temple and the palace. It continues so today.

The innovators exploring the outer reaches of the frontiers of human possibility are the contemplative, mystic and prophetic seers whose vision scans the far horizons of the possible future for humanity and creation. They refuse to buy into the conventional folk wisdom that accepts men and women as violent, greedy, rapacious, needing to be controlled and manipulated for their own good, forever destined to live their lives in hostile and suspicious relationships with one another. In such slavery of the mind and soul one never dares to trust, much less develop, their own innate truth and goodness to claim authority over their own lives. This is true of church communities as well as of individuals. The contemplative, mystic prophet stands in open and direct repudiation of the conventional worship of violence and competition to proclaim nonviolence, poverty of spirit, obedience to the inner truth of divine wisdom embedded in the soul of each person on earth. Their understanding is nourished by the deep living waters of human consciousness. They are emboldened and energized by the insatiable thirst to touch the possible and awaken others to the possibilities within themselves. Consequently they are a threat to those invested in maintaining stability and cultural serenity. Growth occurs within a tension of opposites. To refuse to encounter the tension is to close our hearts to possibilities for growth. Insofar as each of us encounters the challenge and the risk, the human race and our institutions are opened to new possibilities, whether they want to be or not.

In the face of our modern dilemmas, as a radical antidote to the present day cry of the people, you and I stand on the forward edge of a tradition that is a living and always creative process, inexhaustible in its potential to bring light from darkness, life out of death, harmony out of chaos. Darkness, death, chaos are seen to be essential elements in the creation of the order that reveals divine wisdom. Again, it must be recalled, that with the creation of man and woman, the process of the harmonization of creation becomes the human-divine enterprise. When man and woman establish themselves as the center of their own universe, the overall creative process falls under the tryanny of isolated egos, each seeking to establish its own omnipotent reign over all it surveys. Even one's loyalties are conditioned by the unspoken expectation that the object of one's loyalty will in turn meet and support mutual expectations for security and comfort. Loyalty on this level is always subject to the erosion of enticing alternatives offering more immediate or seemingly more lasting gratifications. Thus even altruistic notions are subject to the bartering process, currency in the market for security and well-being. The earth, animals, plants and other persons

become mere objects to be used and consumed. Even God, the unknown and unknowable, is drawn into the constricted realm of our unenlightened minds and self-propelled wills. God and religion become
objects, among many others, in our gallery of goods to be consumed in
the nourishment of our empty hearts.

Jesus, the humble teacher of nonviolence, of the unlimited forgiveness of one's enemies, the one who repudiated all forms of personal
power as well as allegiance to its institutional forms, stands in history
as God's definitive statement of the absolute truth of men and women.
Through his life and actions, as well as his nonviolent acceptance of
death at the hands of religious and political authorities, there emerges a
new and revolutionary vision of what is possible when our sense of self
is grounded in an awareness of, and trust in, the core of radical goodness and truth that is ours by virtue of our participation in God's life.
To live one's life grounded in the heart-center where divine life flows
into history is to live in the mind and heart of Christ. Jesus becomes
more than a mere object of pious devotion, but the model of what
human life can be when freed from the boundaries of a culturally-conditioned sense of the self. In Christ the personal ego is established in its
truth to become the mediating organ of a self united to divine truth.
"That you may be filled with the utter fullness of God" is not Paul's
idle wish. It is a clear vision of one who has discovered the ultimate
possibility for humanity.

It was when they were shaken free of reliance on conventional wisdom, unquestioning allegiance to an institutionalized version of salvation, that the followers of Christ were open to receive the mighty inpouring and outpouring of God's own Holy Spirit. When the first
group of hapless and beleaguered followers finally realized what had
happened to Jesus, and to them, they became an empowered people,
renewed and transformed. This transformation of self-awareness drove
them into the world to reveal this truth to all without regard to religious
or political affiliation, economic or social class, free or slave, man or
woman, saint or sinner.

If the great heroes and heroines, the great epochs of salvation history
reveal our foundational myth telling us who we are, what we are doing
and what our destiny is, Jesus is the one who most fully makes this

truth operative at the core of one human life. That life is paradigmatic of all human life and destiny. Jesus is the fullest enfleshment and actualization of that myth. Thus, his life, word and action, his death and resurrection reveal to each of us, uniquely and personally, the innermost longing and possibility of our lives. Each of us stands in time, and in our place, as a new possibility for humanity. As we open ourselves to the possibility impregnated in our body-mind-spirit being, we stand as lights to a world in darkness. We point the way to new possibilities for all humanity. When church is alive and functioning from its true source, its teachings, rituals and celebrations touch the heart of the people and awaken them to their call to encounter the Christ-event in all its transforming power. When this happens, church is a gathering of persons radically and uncompromisingly committed to the pursuit of the fulfillment of this event in time. In such a community, the world sees a gathering of people freed from the bondage to superficial values and allegiances, not counting the cost nor fearing the consequences. They are surrendered to a vision of what is possible for creation and humanity and their lives are spent in the pursuit of its realization.

In baptism we have been initiated into the Paschal Mystery, and invited to gather that mystery into our self-understanding, and stand in the world, in history, as a new creation, a new possibility for humanity, a doorway opening to a new heaven and a new earth. Here! Now!

Chapter 12

Balance:
In Darkness, Light; in Sin, Grace

Early in life we develop a preference for functioning either in the internal realm of ideas, imagination, dreams and possibilities, that is to say, as introverts, or, as extroverts, we prefer to function in the outer world of action: dynamic, concrete, and focused engagement. For the latter, action is the preferred way of bringing about change, of making things work. In the former, life is energized and restored, stress reduced, by withdrawal to an inner world of ideas and dreams, visions and images containing the seed of new possibilities. For the extrovert, life is restored, boredom and fatigue overcome by activity and social engagement. The problem is not that of one being better than the other, but in favoring and cultivating one while devaluing and neglecting the other.

The unhappy result for the exaggerated introvert, energized and restored by withdrawal from activity, is an inner life disengaged from the nitty-gritty of social contact. The inner life is often unrealistic, spacy, romantic and irrelevant. The one who overdevelops the inner realm to the exclusion of the outer finds him or herself inadequate and clumsy when seeking to cope with life's problems and challenges. A common defense is to debunk the importance of the lived experience, the concrete problems demanding attention, while falling back on theoretical and abstract theories, dreams and visions having little or no relevance to the real experience of persons struggling in the heat and fury of life's battles. The exaggerated introvert can become the victim of his or her own easy access to ideas, fantasies and dreams, believing this to be the only true or worthwhile reality.

The extrovert, on the other hand, may present the opposite excess, feeling nervous, anxious and threatened when confronted with life's inevitable encounters with solitude or isolation. Because activity and engagement are so rewarding and life-giving for the extrovert, the danger of avoiding healthy encounters with one's inner life presents hazards that threaten the overall quality of action. Just as the introvert may debunk the importance of outer engagement, so the exaggerated extrovert may tend to belittle and disdain the movements of the inner world as a frivolous land of fantasy, the refuge of eccentric dreamers, unreal and irrelevant.

Thus, exaggerating one or the other causes us to miss out on the richness and depth of creative engagement with life which is the fruit of a healthy connection to the hidden and unrealized side of the personality.

It is fair to say that most of us underestimate our innate but unrealized riches and potentials, living on the shallow outer edge of our potential for deep and rich spirituality. We deprive ourselves, and others, of the full riches of a life fully lived.

The common task, for the extrovert as well as the introvert, is to harmonize the outer world with the rhythms and flows of our inner life. By integrating our interior life with the exterior, our participation in the seen and unseen dimensions of creation will be nourishing and beneficial to ourselves, to other persons, and to material creation.

To properly understand prayer is to see and experience our devotions, worship, praise, adoration, the celebration of sacrament and liturgy, as disciplined and focused exercises awakening us to the forgotten or undervalued aspect of our personality. This awakening initiates the integration and participation in our conscious life with the hidden depths of our unconscious. Our eyes, ears, mind and heart, are opened to receive the blessings of creation flowing both within and without, from the seen as well as the unseen. To pray is to be awake, to be enlightened, it is to be fully alive to the adventure of life in all its dimensions. The concept of "heart," the "inner" or "hidden self" as the center of our relationship with God is frequent and insistent in Sacred Scripture. "In the abundance of his glory may he, through his Spirit, enable you to grow firm in power with regard to your inner self, so that Christ may live in your hearts through faith" (Eph. 3:16-17 NJB). And think also of the insistence on a listening heart in Hebrews cited above (Heb. 4:12-13). And certainly Jeremiah knew the value of the heart in our relationship with God. "Within them I shall plant my law, writing it on their hearts. Then I shall be their God and they will be my people" (Jer 31:33-34, NJB).

We recall again that an essential quality of prayer is an opening of the mind and heart to God. God is creative, self-giving, and revealing, not only within, but beyond the horizons of our perceptual knowledge. We all have an equally-weighty need to be attentive not to one or the other dimension of our world, but to both the inner and outer, seen and unseen, the dark and the light, what is and what can be. Listening means to be attentive to life; it is to realize that there is no barrier between inner and outer, seen and unseen, but all is one free-flowing reality, one emerging from the other and flowing back again. The task of life is to become aware, fully aware of the unity of being occurring around and within. The heart-center is that deep place where eternity and time, divinity and humanity, the known and the unknowable, light and dark, sin and grace, meet and blend in our fleshed experience. This is the soil out of which our life with the divine is nourished. Our ulti-mate union with the divine is the fruit of our cooperation with God's Spirit, continuing the divine creative act of bringing order to chaos, light to the darkness, life where there seems to be only death.

The contemplative is the one who establishes the unity of the inner life with the outer, the material with the spiritual, allowing full partici-pation in life. The contemplative heart knows no division or distinction between contemplation and/or action, matter and spirit. One flows into and nourishes the other. Moments of silence and solitude deepen and enrich one's active participation in life; one's actions and enterprises add color, tone, and grounding to silence and solitude.

The mystic consciousness is the normal state of awareness in its whole and integral truth. Knowledge of reality is grasped not only by the physical senses, but by the feelings, the intuition and instincts as well. The knowledge of reason joined to the knowledge of the body is to possess the wisdom of the heart-center. And it might be well for us Westerners to remember that the body has its own way of receiving and communicating information, if we would only learn how to listen. The body communicates our innermost secrets to the world around us, as well as receiving and interpreting information without the mediation of our rational faculties. This is the wisdom that opens us to the mystical.

The mystical consciousness is as much a quality of the extrovert as of the introvert. It is a quality of consciousness that takes into account the wisdom of the body as much as the wisdom of our mind and that of the earth. It is the quality of a consciousness fully aware and engaged by the unseen and seen presence of God penetrating material creation, history, and the center of each person. The mystic consciousness knows that our knowledge of God, our theological formulations and dogmas, are but a threshold into the unfathomable mystery of God ultimately unknowable in human terms. The mystic assents to the lonely journey through and beyond the known to a solitary, unique engagement with the Divine. Paradoxically in this solitude of personal union with the Divine, we encounter the fullness of life as our awareness awakens to the realization that all beings have their existence in union with the creator. In union with God, we are one with everything and everyone else. Or, coming at it from the other direction, insofar as we live in harmonious interaction with other persons and material creation, we are in fact enjoying a oneness of being with the creator, even though we may prefer to call it something else.

Prophetic energy is released when the walls of resistance between our inner and outer life, our body knowledge and rational knowledge, are dismantled. The introvert and extrovert stand together at this threshold where the inner life is nourished and strengthened by the flesh of uncompromising reality; the external concrete reality is nourished, deepened, and given balance by its rootedness in the transcendent life of the heart-center. Engagement with the outer world, for the extrovert no less than the introvert, is deepened and enriched by intuition, feelings, and instincts enlarging and enlightening our sense perceptions and rational knowing.

If integration and harmony of the exterior and interior life are the desired goals for the serious seeker, then we cannot afford to take for granted assumptions about our participation in either realm. The extroverted person may be just as deluded by unfounded assumptions and unconscious biases surrounding the life of action as he or she might be about the life of interior prayer. The same can be said for the introvert and unquestioned assumptions about the value of the inner life, as well as about unquestioned biases about action and apostolic engagement. Truth and wisdom lie in integration and balance, opening up heretofore unrealized dimensions for all.

The principle we are discussing can be stated quite simply: The outer life of action and relationship is deepened and enhanced to the extent that it is rooted in one's life of the spirit: the interior or heart-center. One's life of the spirit, the interior, or heart-center, is proportionately enriched and energized to the extent that it is opened and influenced by external reality. If either dimension is cut off, or in any way denied access to the other, our spirituality, and all that goes with it, suffers from a lack of grounding in reality.

The excessively introverted person remains, in his or her superficial interiority, naively unaware that the sin and disorder of the external world which they find so intrusive and disconcerting to their inner life, is but a reflection of their own deep interior condition. The compulsive extrovert fails to recognize in her or his restless busyness the symptoms of inner emptiness at the heart of so much of the violence and social malaise of our time. For all of us, redemption and integration, peace grounded in reality, awaits us in the very place we seek to avoid.

When our hearts and minds are opened to God, we first become aware of our own ache for union and the poverty of the empty promises of our unredeemed world. As we become more humbled by the awareness of our inner poverty, more chastened by the awareness of our reliance on idols and their tyranny over our lives, we begin to recognize that the sinfulness of the world we live in is an echo of the cry of our heart. In prayer our lives become the meeting place between divine compassion and a world in darkness. Because we know that the sin of the world resides in our hearts, we bring compassion and the good news of redemption where before we brought judgment and condemnation.

Christ was obviously every bit as comfortable with sinners as with saints. Why? When he embraced our humanity, he took on all of it, the dark as well as the light. He did not disdain the unseemly frailty of the human condition but entered fully into our condition in order that through that condition he might reveal its promise for union with the divine. When Jesus encountered the prostitute, the "sinner," so maligned and despised, the blind, the lame and the lepers, his peace and healing power emerged from a consciousness aware of, and at peace with, the seeds of the same reality within his own human flesh (2 Cor. 5:21). While Christ did not "sin," he understood sin because he took to himself our human flesh and all that was included in that mystery. If the Incarnation of God in human flesh is to mean anything to us today, we need to remember that it was the totality of the human fleshed existence that was raised to full union with God through Christ on the cross. Jesus is the "way" through which we, from the midst of our earthy existence, make our journey to our full participation in divinity. Just as God, through Jesus, fully participated in our humanity, so do we, through Jesus, fully regain our participation in the divine. This is not a dream of some future, disconnected existence in some disconnected place, but is to be fully actualized in our lives and actions, our human relationships, here, now.

A person grounded in contemplation plumbs the depths of his or her own sinfulness and experiences the healing touch of Divine Mercy. The word of compassion and mercy brought to others has first taken flesh in their own heart. The preacher of the word, rooted in contemplation, is speaking the word that has taken flesh in his or her own life. In short, contemplative prayer makes us first of all the sacrament of the mysteries we proclaim. For Paul, this meant reconciliation. To be reconciled to God is to be the righteousness of God through Christ (2 Cor. 5:17-21). Christ did not hold anyone's sins against them, but drew them from that human reality into a new relationship with God and, therefore, with themselves.

Some reflection aimed at deepening our understanding of the dynamics of silence and solitude might be helpful. A fundamental place to start is to remember that silence and solitude are not static, empty, or lifeless realities with no purpose or function other than to fulfill a religious mandate imposed by arbitrary divine or human will. Silence and solitude have always been experienced as dynamic and creative moments of encounter with transcendent realities, piercing human consciousness with expanded awareness. Expanded awareness moves in all directions. Our center of awareness remains the heart-center, but the horizons expand outward to embrace larger dimensions of reality to make it one's own, and inward to deeper levels of self-awareness and self-possession. Our self-awareness now includes an experiential awareness of our life sharing in the eternal divine life of God. In this union with divine life we enjoy union with all creation. We become more profoundly aware that we participate not only in the sin and brokenness of creation, but likewise we share in its potential and promise of union with the divine. At the same time, as inner awareness deepens, consciousness of the outer world opens to the realization that the condition of humanity and creation has its roots deep within particular human souls. One awakens to the reality that to be alive is really an experience of what Thich Nhat Han, the Vietnamese Buddhist poet and peace activist, refers to as "interbeing" with all creation and with its uncreated source.

To relate the experience of God to others, the mystics of our tradition have employed the imagery of wind, storm, earthquake, lightening, and thunder. Certainly not experiences to be taken lightly and far removed from much of the serendipitous blather surrounding many contemporary notions of God as buddy, sugar daddy, or celestial Santa Claus.

In contrast to these innocuous folk conventions, we have Matthew's use of the word *seismos*, earthquake, to describe those moments in which people were confronted with a realization that Jesus was the Son of God, their savior; the one who came to reveal truth, to bring light to darkness; to dismantle the tyranny that oppressed human spirits. Paul Hinnebusch presents an enlightening study of Matthew's use of the word "earthquake" in his gospel (*St. Matthew's Earthquake: Judgment and Discipleship in the Gospel of Matthew*, Servant Books, 1980). In Matthew's story of Palm Sunday, he uses *seismos* to describe the stirring, the shaking, as if by an "earthquake," that ran through the populace (Mt. 21:10). Again in 8:24, Matthew replaces the word "squall" with the word meaning earthquake, a seismic shaking reaching from the depths of the sea to the heights of the heavens. In Psalm 18, the storms of Israel were described as so violent that they caused even the heavens to shake with fury. "The very springs of ocean were exposed, the world's foundations were laid bare, at your roaring, Yahweh, at the blast of breath from your nostrils!" (Ps. 18:15 NJB). In the popular mind, earthquakes and storms became the stock symbol for divine manifestations. Our biblical tradition reminds us that an encounter with God can be hazardous to our accustomed way of seeing things. Everything, even our cherished religious conventions, our political security, are at risk. It is significant that when the Lord invited his disciples to follow him, he took them into the midst of this "sky shaking," "earth shattering" storm that scared them out of their wits. It was from this soul-shaking encounter with Jesus' authority over the primal forces of untamed nature that their hearts were opened to ask themselves who this man could be. Their assumptions about who he was and the true nature of his mission were beginning to weaken. This simple man, Jesus, had more to him than at first met the eye. Matthew is describing the process by which Jesus bored through the structures of their popular messianic conditioning, preparing the way for its ultimate collapse at his crucifixion and death.

There is another earthquake at the moment of his death (27:52), and at the Resurrection (28:2). In case the point might have been missed, let us remember that earthquakes have an awesome and disconcerting power to disestablish what human efforts have taken great pains to establish. This is just as true in our personal inner life as it is in the physical world. When the soul awakens to the presence of God, everything is at stake, everything! Temple and palace are alike called to judgment along with everything else that might provide our life with security and stability. That which can bend and yield will prove the stronger. Roots running deep provide a firm anchor. The unbending, the brittle, the rigid, the superficial will perish.

The shaking of the ground was only a paltry shadow of the shaking and dismantling of the soul that took place in the hapless, frightened, and weary followers. That dismantling not only struck the final death blow to their egocentric expectations of messianic salvation, but likewise gave birth to a new self-understanding that freed them from the shackles of conventional wisdom with the constricted temple religion that bound their spirits. A power was released from within them that has been shaking, challenging, and confronting our favored assumptions and delusions ever since. Matthew leaves little room to doubt the seriousness of an encounter with the living God. Jesus invites us into the earthquake and storm in order that we might be shaken, tipped over and emptied, to enter into his death and resurrection. The destruction of the established, conventional structures, either within our own hearts, or in society, brings about the new order. With the accumulation of our modern day biases, with their religious and cultural delusions reaching critical mass, can another spiritual earthquake rearranging the structures of our self-understanding be far off?

Perhaps the trivialization and miniaturization of the Incarnate revelation of Divine Wisdom in Jesus are the causes of our spiritual malaise today. When we have a God that is no bigger than our attaché case, who remains cozily distant and comfortably contained in monstrances and guilded tabernacles, who remains entombed in archaic formulations and literal interpretations of the Word, who is praised through rote recitations, is satisfied with empty adherence to conventional behavior and self-serving cultural virtues, is available to our beck and call, we are left with a god no larger than our culturally-conditioned self-understanding. We are left with no vision larger than our own horizons, no expectations to stretch and enlarge our self-understanding, no hope stretching our vision beyond our present hopelessness and cynical violence against one another and creation. We are stuck with a god who is simply the reflection of our own shadow on the wall. All the while we long for a god who will shake us to the bone, pierce us to our center, and awaken us to the true potential of our humanity. Rabbi Abraham Heschel, a modern-day mystic, was commenting on the quality of religion during his day some 20 years ago when he stated: "One is embarrassed to be called religious in the face of religion's failure to keep alive the image of God in the face of man . . . Little does religion ask from contemporary man. It is ready to offer comfort; it has no courage to challenge. It is ready to offer edification; it has no courage to break idols, to shatter the callousness. The trouble is that religion has become 'religion'—institution, dogma, securities. It is not an event anymore. Its acceptance involves no risk, no strain. Our greatest danger is not lack of faith, but the vulgarization of faith." (Quoted in "Sequoia," News of Religion in the World, October-November 1989).

Today, some 20 years later, the words of this wise man seem even more apropos.

Our prophets, mystics, doers and shakers, those who vigorously challenge our pat assumptions—religious and secular—often came upon their vocation reluctantly and unwillingly through unforeseen, unwanted and unexpected encounters with God. Their call to service was often discerned through the prism of the experience of failure, betrayal, sin, and human weakness. In the course of their daily pursuits, they were often rudely awakened to the realization that their accustomed religious symbols and images had lost the power to penetrate their heart and awaken them to, and then address, their fundamental human questions.

It is possible to discern two paths to the center capable of bringing about the upheaval and dismantling that gives birth to the spirit of poverty necessary for conversion and transformation that prepares the soul for union with the Divine. The first, most painful route taken by many is the involuntary encounter with our self-deception. Throughout life we struggle to find meaning and significance. All too often we do this at the expense of losing touch with our center. We gain the world at the expense of losing our soul. The warning of the Gospel becomes all too true in our lives. Discouragement, depression, a loss of purpose and meaning haunt us, eroding our mental as well as our physical health. Divorce, sickness or other symptoms of our dis-ease eat away at the quality of our lives. If we are lucky, or alert to the signals coming to our consciousness, we might take the time and make the effort to reevaluate and get back in touch with reality before more serious trouble erupts. Unfortunately, too many ignore the signals, or are too caught up in frenzied activities to even notice them. The frantic pace we set ourselves is a vain attempt to "get with it," pay our entrance dues into the club. Thus our activities override the early warning signals. Finally, we collapse in a heap, burned out, disgusted, shamed at our inability to make our life make sense. For these persons, reality dawns as they lie on their sick bed, or watch a marriage or career, sometimes both, go down the drain. They played by the rules, lived by the book; still, life is in ruins. They have been betrayed by the very system they dedicated their life to. This is as true for clergy and religious as it is for corporate executives.

Today it is not uncommon to encounter elderly clergy, as well as religious men and women who, after a lifetime in ministry, face their later years in empty and arid restlessness, regretting the loss of vigor, facing the so called "golden years" with fear and bitterness. They have labored long and faithfully, but their souls have been starved, denied the rich nourishment of a deep interior life of contemplation. What should be a time of grateful repose, the age of the wise mother or father, is instead often a time of sorrow. Many feel rejected, cast aside, no longer useful, a burden to their community. What should be a time of prayerful preparation and joyful anticipation of one's final surrender into the fullness of life is instead a time of sorrow and apprehension. This, unfortunately, is the bitter fruit of a value system that has placed more emphasis on works accomplished than on being.

The other path is the contemplative path of remaining sensitive and alert to the balance and harmony between one's external, lived experience and the inner rhythms of the true, core self. This attention to the inner life keeps one in touch with those delicate messages from within, enabling one to keep things in perspective, balanced between the inner and outer demands of healthy human living.

Both paths bring us to the point which Paul speaks of as "putting on the mind and heart of Christ," or experiencing the reality of union he describes by saying: "I live now, not I, but Christ lives in me" (Gal 2:20). Both of these paths thrust one into an honest encounter with fundamental questions concerning the meaning of life and death. These events, voluntary and involuntary, uncompromisingly and bluntly confront us with the shallowness and poverty of our best, but often misguided, efforts to bring meaning to our life.

The disciples were dragged unwillingly to the cross. There they experienced the stripping away of their cherished religious beliefs, their hopes for a political and religious restoration according to their plan. From this nightmare, a new religious consciousness was born.

Meaning is sought and reached through our encounter with meaninglessness. Contemplative prayer is the voluntary and disciplined effort to maintain our life on a balanced, harmonious and life-giving path that enables each day to be an opportunity to strengthen our grounding in truth. By means of a regular contemplative discipline, we deliberately look meaninglessness in the face and find the spirit of poverty that frees us to seek meaning that transcends life and death. Contemplative prayer is a faithful and regular way to find truth before it finds us.

The contemplative path, as we shall later elaborate on, leads to peace, but first it leads one into an awareness of the lack of true peace, the false peace of cheap security in false assumptions and shallow allegiances. The awakening process leads through a process of dismantling of these structures, often leaving one with a momentary loss of certitude, a disorientation with a corresponding sense of futility. This is the path into the deep center traveled by our great Mothers and Fathers of the Faith. In our time of immediate gratification and painless surgery, quick conversions and the serendipitous certitude of fundamentalist religion, the true contemplative seeker is a solitary traveler.

Chapter 13

Solitude:
The End of Boundaries

Prayer understood as a search for truth, a dialogue with the events of our life, is based on the faith conviction that Divine Wisdom is encountered in the day-to-day events of our life. This Divine Wisdom is often obscured or lost because we are spiritually numbed due to our need to plunge into the enterprise of creating a self we believe will gain affirmation and a sense of security from our world.

Our dialogue with God includes a notion of truth residing within our inner self, the true self that is a reflection of divine wisdom. This is the basis of our tradition of desert, mountain, and wilderness, images used to describe the human quest for the Divine—or is it a surrender to the Divine pursuit of the human? All religious traditions include the practice of withdrawing from normal human engagement to heed more closely the movements of the Divine resonating within the soul. Essential to this notion of authentic withdrawal and disengagement is an understanding that it is not a rejection or an abandonment of human social enterprise, but rather a more intense listening to the signs of the times that impact on, and have their resonances deep within, the soul. The rhythm of withdrawal and return, a breathing in and a breathing out, complements and deepens one's engagement with life, making our participation more redemptive and healing. On this basis, withdrawal is a healthy attempt to fine-tune one's relationship with ultimate concerns, of bringing into clearer focus the core values influencing one's life. It is by attending to the integrity of this fundamental relationship that all other relationships fall into their proper perspective.

If the core values that drive one's life are determined by social conditioning rather than responsible choices, it follows that all other relationships will reflect the conventional social mores. Thus if one's main concern is the acquisition and preservation of personal power, prestige, and the material accouterments that go with these, all other values such as loyalty, family relationships and relationships with God will be modified to accommodate themselves to these values. In this case, one's relationship to God is not determined by creeds professed, religious rituals performed, but by the unconscious motivating force of maintaining one's unreflective value system intact. The religious fervor of a nation is not determined by the numbers attending Sunday services, but by the value system that drives them from Sunday afternoon until Saturday evening. Money spent on weapons of war, in hedonistic and self-gratifying commodities, reveals more about the state of our soul than Sunday services. Our uncritical willingness to sacrifice tens of thousands of young lives in the defense of our consumerism, and our fear-ridden compulsion to impose our rule on other nations reveals more about the condition of our cultural psyche than our ability to quote scripture and attend prayer meetings and theology classes.

By withdrawal into solitude and silence, one gains a clearer vision and deeper commitment to essentials. Silent solitude is the dark, generative side of action; action in authentic relationships is silence and solitude coming into daylight, its completion in creative, prophetic engagement. It leads to harmonious living in which one's external engagements are in tune with one's inner sense of self and purpose. False values and inauthentic goals are seen for what they are and replaced by allegiance to the one God and the pursuit of enlightened core values in harmony with one's sense of self.

In silence and solitude the soul most unambiguously encounters the presence of the Divine and the truths surrounding our understanding of the Divine. This mysterious region beyond the reach of the immediate din and clatter of social engagement, beneath the neatly-woven barriers of our own ego defenses, is where the Divine speaks freely and uncensored to the heart. Personal silence surrounded by unembellished solitude is the moment of primal truth. The most immediate contact with God's revelation occurs from within our personal and utterly unique existence. This experience of the deep self becomes the soil into which God's Word, alive and active, can reveal the central meaning of one's life and begin the purification and transformation leading to union with God.

Thus, John the Baptist, a desert dweller, was open and vulnerable to Divine Wisdom awakening his heart to the plight of the people. In his heart, like that of Moses, echoed the cry of the people rising to God. The pain of the people and the righteousness of God met and joined as one in his heart, igniting prophetic energy. Filled and anointed with Divine indignation, John's message went to the heart of his listeners, one of whom responded by removing John's head. Through John's preaching, nourished in the solitude of the desert, God's Word cut and opened the heart of his hearers.

So too, the Spirit of God led Jesus into the wilderness to look into the face of the demons holding sway over the heart of humanity. From the wilderness experience of Jesus emerged the vision of a new humanity articulated in Matthew's Gospel in the Sermon on the Mount, chapters 5-7. Or more succinctly in Luke's use of the passage from Is. 61:1-2 (Lk 4:14-22). An encounter with the Divine is an awakening and sensitizing to our deep inner self, the true self which is a participation in the divine self. In that deep encounter we become aware of our responsibility for, and our participation in the sin and the healing of history. With Moses we stand thunderstruck before the burning bush, hearing our call to summon forth the inner strength to confront the Pharaoh. With Mary our confused soul asks, "How this can be?" With repeated immersions, habituating ourselves in contemplative prayer, our evasiveness and defenses weaken until, with Moses and Mary and legions after them, we hesitantly and reluctantly take the first fragile steps into prophetic living. We know that to not act is to participate in the lie that oppresses the human spirit. Our superficial peace has been taken; there is no way to go now but forward to the total self-giving of the Cross. We glimpse our own call, a sense of purpose, a reason for our life, our suffering, our dreams and longings. Our personal sinfulness is placed within a larger context of our mutual participation with humanity and creation in a shared struggle to stretch towards as-yet-unrealized, dimly-intuited possibilities.

Within the light of our biblical tradition, we grasp a notion of sin as being on the edge of creative promise of new possibilities for creation.

To sin is to refuse to respond to our call to become what it is possible to become, to refuse to do what we feel and know needs to be done. In psychological terms, sin is the refusal to embrace the task of inner growth and development, with its external expression in responsible action. We allow the tyranny of human respect to prevent us from appropriating the authority to make responsible and free choices. Grace is actualized in the acceptance of our call to carry our weight in bringing history and creation to their appointed end. To this end, our common vocation is to become fully human by being fully and responsibly free and open to the possibilities hidden within our inner self. A "Yes" to purpose and mission is uttered concurrently with a resounding "No" to the selfish non-essentials and self-centered preoccupations that have heretofore cluttered our lives and actions.

Jesus' bold and unambiguous "No" to the Evil One in the wilderness was at the same time a "Yes" to a way of simplicity and nonviolence, a life of service and humility that, in his "No," stopped the evil tyranny dead in its tracks. The "No" to the seductions of the Evil One enabled his spirit to remain free, even to surrender to failure and human weakness, the loss of everything he had worked for, rather than react in kind to human minds and actions sealed in darkness. Our "Yes" to the simplicity of Gospel values, with a corresponding "No" to the unredeemed values that hold the world in bondage and which are now seen in our heart, is the beginning of the dissolution and ultimate destruction of the power of sin and its sway over the human soul.

This episode in the wilderness is a dramatic preview of the ensuing encounters and repudiations of these evils as they were encountered subtly insinuating themselves into the relationships and decisions of Jesus and his disciples. They struggled to live and interact within the circumstances of their environment, to sort out right from wrong, and to live according to the truth as it was being revealed in Jesus. Jesus set himself on a path that would lead to his death and the loss of his plans and visions of a new order established in the hearts of his followers. By so doing, he gave force to his "No" to the Evil One in the wilderness. He allowed his mission and vision of a new order to succumb to the forces of evil rather than yield to compromise. This radical living out of his mission shocked, dismayed and perhaps angered his followers.

At the same time it punched through the defensive, self-serving barriers of the conventional expectations of the Messiah. They were left vulnerable, naked and raw, to ponder the meaning of the disheartening event of the crucifixion and death of their leader and the loss of all that he had promised.

The temptations in the wilderness and the cross on Calvary are connected by a thread of daily encounters with the tyranny of the evil ruling in the hearts of men and women, revealed in countless ways in our actions and decisions. The frail sensitivity of the fine points of a life of harmony, truth and beauty are all but washed aside as we embark on our daily pursuit of security, approval and approbation from our world and its values. Both our consciousness and our consciences are daily and even hourly numbed by glib rationalizations sealing our heart, deafening us, blinding us to our call to be prophetically holy, to be countercultural. We convince ourselves that conventional mediocrity is an acceptable norm, that the world has no place for religious values or virtue that repudiate the conventions of society. We nervously argue ourselves free from taking the Gospel too seriously, lest it interfere with our security and well-laid plans. True religious commitment and unflinching prophetic living give way to comfortable religious conventions, enabling us to maintain the pretense without suffering a corresponding change in attitudes and values. We cage our demons in the unconscious, we ignore our call to heroism and holiness and hunker down into restless mediocrity. In this unconsciousness, the power of darkness continues its reign in history. Into the unconscious we tightly pack our repressed fears, our naked greed and lust, our rage. Beneath the thin surface of our public selves, these demons lurk, sabotaging our relationships, our decisions, our health and overall well-being. Even our worship becomes one more self-cleansing ritual designed to sustain and strengthen our social image.

Like the disciples before us, if we allow ourselves a moment of vulnerability, of honest questioning, we too will be confronted by the outrageous affront of the Cross, challenging our easy assumptions and evasions. If Jesus calls us to peace and the joy of the Reign of Wisdom, that reality is achieved by the dismantling of everything we have allowed to reign in our hearts that is contrary to the truth of ourselves.

It is a sad irony, as well as a self-defeating contradiction, that much modern religion promotes a style of virtue that is a flight from the truth of our hidden selves, a flight away from the very place where we encounter our grace hidden within the debris of our sin. The episode of the wilderness calls us to look at the uncensored reality of evil, the evil that bonds us to its seductive will. By identifying and owning our bondage, we will find the energy to utter our radical "No" that is at the same time a "Yes" to our forgotten, hidden truth. It is an uncomfortable paradox of our belief that our journey to God leads directly into the face of the Evil One, our journey into peace takes us through the storm and chaos of our unredeemed inner self, our journey into our truth leads us into the idolatrous lies holding our decisions in bondage.

The temptations in the wilderness are a paradigm of the soul's encounter with the tyranny of sin active in the darkness of our hidden self. As we glibly go about our daily business, the tiny, silent seeds of self interest, fear, the need for approval, success, the pursuit of our personal egocentric immortality silently leak out to poison and otherwise taint even our most seemingly-innocent actions and decisions.

Prayer, when allowed to penetrate the layers of defenses surrounding our heart-center, disconcertingly sensitizes us to the presence and power of sin in our heart, its all-pervading insidious influence in our most innocent actions. In the wilderness temptations, immediately after the Baptism and before his entry into public ministry, Jesus leads us into a fearless encounter with this evil, opens the way for a new life grounded in a vision of a new possibility for humanity. We are invited to follow Him into a life that clearly and courageously, through the centuries of our historical journey to the present, and now actualized in each of our lives, continues to identify and repudiate the influence of sin on a daily basis. If we want to trace the evils of history to their source, we are led into the center of our self where the sin of humanity and the sin of history live and are nourished in our daily actions and decisions. History and humanity are healed and brought to redemptive light as we allow our shared sin to be revealed and identified within our own deep self. To find our grace, we need to encounter our sin. The transformation of history begins with the conversion and subsequent transformation of one's heart.

One dare not invite the "sinner" to be converted without a humble and serene acceptance of personal participation in sin. The wisdom of self- knowledge—the fruit of the deep prayer of the heart—opens the eyes of the soul to see in the frightened, hardened and cynical eyes of the prostitute one's own propensity to infidelity to truth. The same for the rapist, child molester, murderer and so on until we reach the outer limits of the outcast and rejected of our society, the biblical leper. Authentic prayer helps us realize and accept the fact that we are all connected at the heart-center to a common spiritual hunger. It is this common spiritual hunger that joins the sinner to the saint. As prayer leads deeper and deeper into the hidden inner self, the true self lost and forgotten beneath the debris of our personal idols, one embraces the paradoxes of sin and grace within his or her self. In one's personal knowledge and acceptance of sin is discovered the soil from which grace grows into humble, compassionate and healing love.

Compassionate love, the fruit of an open and humble soul, is not the safe antiseptic love of the clinician shrouded behind professional objectivity and detachment, or of the theologian formulated in rituals and dogmas. It is the love that allows the soil and messiness, the unmanageable untidiness of life to invade and disrupt our set agendas. It is the inconvenient vulnerability of the Samaritan who could not find it within his heart to hide behind rationalizations, clinical objectivity, or theological distinctions and evasions. His life was swayed from its set path, his pocketbook was invaded, its contents depleted, by the plight of his brother.

Living the evangelical life is essentially a commitment to a life of deepening sensitivity to shades and nuances in the decisions involved in our daily lives. This is the fruit of daily deep, still, listening prayer, opening the mind and heart to God creating from within the evolving consciousness of human beings. Consciousness unfolding beyond the safe dimensions of our isolated ego, to embrace the lives of others, is the creation of the body of Christ—the reign of Holy Wisdom made up of persons bonded together in an awareness of the organic unity and singleness of life in the life of the One God.

To not be prayerful is to be insensitive to life on all levels; it is to live in a numb slumber, ignorantly unaware of the deep dimensions of life. To put it another way, insensitivity, narrowness of interest, living within a tightly woven, self-absorbed life is a sure sign of a lack of prayer, even in the midst of a flurry of religious observances. It is impossible to live deeply the evangelical life without this daily, disciplined rootedness in deep, listening prayer that startles and disconcerts as it awakens our soul to its participation in the fullness of life. This full participation is not without a humble recognition of one's share in the plight of humanity, including sin.

The imagery of the desert place, the mountaintop, or the wilderness does not call to a specific material place, but rather invites us to the silence and solitude of the heart, untamed, wild, chaotic, not yet knowing the light and order promised by our redeemer. Consequently, stillness, silence, solitude bring forth restlessness, anxiety, guilt, and a variety of other forms of uneasiness. The alienated ego knows that its defenses are being encroached upon, its rule is being challenged.

As we attempt this deep silent prayer of surrender, we might experience some stress or discomfort and settle for anxiety-reducing ploys, reaching for something to do, some way to maintain control. Even spiritual reading or "saying" prayers might serve to anesthetize the heart feeling the stress of unrequited silence, naked solitude. But, for all its pious dress, it is ultimately a taking control, a reassertion of our agenda, a flight from the distress of our encounter with our unknown, forgotten self. Our will is reengaged to relieve us of the anxiety of our solitary encounter with our inner demons.

This restlessness is a smoke screen sent forth by our ego to confuse and dismay us. The route to deeper prayer is not away from, but courageously through the smoke screen. Our tradition invites us to employ disciplined methods of maintaining physical and inner stillness by focusing our attention on the breath and a sacred word. Rather than turning and running, we maintain our stance. We allow our demons to show their face, to be named and seen for what they are. Concentrating on our breathing and sacred word enable us to sit and allow the thoughts, the feelings, the images to be ventilated, given their freedom.

In the initial stages of our efforts we are likely to experience more recent memories accompanied by feelings of hurt, anger, fear or resentment. We might be flooded by forgotten hurts and angers or failures sometimes accompanied by waves of long-forgotten feelings. By sitting calmly, praying our chosen sacred word, concentrating on our breath, we invite their uncensored presence and acknowledge them as participants in our salvation history. In trust we surrender them to a benign wisdom that knows how to draw light from darkness, life from death, grace from sin.

The dynamic at work is that the ego is disengaged, left unemployed, and therefore no longer able to process and filter out matter offensive and unacceptable to the conscious mind and the public self. Our ego is charged with the task of keeping from consciousness anything in our personality that contradicts our carefully-crafted public image. This process is aided by engagement in activities and tasks aimed at enhancing the establishment, promotion and preservation of the public self. The most fundamental act of homage to the Divine is to humbly receive into consciousness our sinfulness. The false self is immolated in an act of profound humility in order that the true self can begin to live. This is the truest meaning of the biblical injunction, "to die in order that we might live."

In the Christian tradition, the ego is not destroyed, but freed to be the organ of true self-awareness, mediating our deepest and most authentic self to the world in which we live. The ego is freed from its defensive role and allowed to mediate the Christ-self in unqualified service to all, without counting the cost. The person fully realizes the human potential to become a sacrament of God's presence in history.

Chapter 14

The Heart Center:
Sinful Saints; Saintly Sinners

The public self is fabricated to misrepresent, hiding as much as it reveals. While it reveals one's more or less successful effort at constructing a personality and style of life that mimics the values, attitudes and mores promoted by society, by the same token it hides those qualities of one's personality that undermine or do not substantiate the kind of self one wants to promote.

Carl Jung referred to this hidden side of our personality as the Shadow. The Shadow is essentially the collected material containing those aspects of our personality that we do not want others to know about us, or that we do not want to know about ourselves. It includes the hidden fears, anxieties, sexual impulses, and rages that we have learned to fear for one reason or another. In short, the Shadow is the hiding place of everything we have learned is "not nice." This material is repressed below our conscious awareness so that we forget that it is an integral part of our human nature revealing itself in our particular personality. We effectively "forget" who we are and live on the fragile shell of a fabricated personality. We have disavowed and alienated a segment of our personality from conscious participation in life, and in so doing stepped aside from our participation in the human experience. Jung calls this aspect of the unconscious the "personal unconscious" to distinguish it from the "collective unconscious," which contains elements which we share in common with the human species.

This unconscious but dynamic and active pool of forgotten matter becomes the source of much of our neurotic anxiety and fear, leading to the subtle erosion of the quality of our participation in life. In its most benign form, it deceives us into thinking that we are free from the sins and shortcomings that afflict others. We fall into the trap of believing that we are something other than we really are. We look with dismay and consternation at those who more dramatically and tragically suffer from symptoms of human frailty which we are unaware of in ourselves. In a more virulent expression of this self-ignorance, one projects righteous wrath onto those who fail to measure up and embody one's standard of behavior. The drug addict or alcoholic, the criminal, sometimes the elderly, the disabled and homeless are subtly despised as being inadequate, careless and irresponsible. It is our egotistic way of separating ourselves from those realities of our environment that haunt us, because they stir up faint echoes of uncertainty about an aspect of ourselves we are out of touch with.

When this repressed matter is perceived as sin, we compound the issue by adding the pain of guilt, shame, or the fear of damnation. This judgmental attitude adds to the intensity of our fear and dislike of our designated "sinners," but it likewise makes it doubly difficult to face up to these realities in ourselves. This fear simply adds fuel to our repression and consequent unconscious projection onto others.

Projection in and of itself is neither good nor bad, but our unconscious projections prevent us from recognizing those aspects of our hidden self. As long as the projection remains unconscious, we are shrouded in a self-serving amnesia. If this unconscious projection is not revealed for what it truly is, that is, brought to consciousness, it is likely that the lost part of our soul will ambush us from the unconscious, trip us and land us on our face.

Thus the homophobic male who rants against the homosexual may well find himself, at some point in his life, dealing with frighteningly graphic fantasies and temptations to the same behavior he finds so hateful in others. He might find himself in alliances that previously would have seemed inconceivable. Or, because of his repressed sexual feelings, relationships with other males may become so anxiety-producing, fraught with guilt and suspicion, that true male bonding, so necesssary for a full affective life, may be impossible. No one is free from sin; we just have different ways of manifesting that commonly-shared aspect of our humanity. The public stance of so many clergy, including, and perhaps most especially celibate clergy, vis-a-vis sexual sins, while appearing to be firmly established in traditional ethics and morals, is more probably a defensive measure by which they publicly disavow and distance themselves from behavior that comes perilously close to awakening them to a repressed part of their own pyschic life.

It is sadly ironic—poetic justice?—that our church, so repressive in areas of sexuality is now faced with a stream of sexual scandals among the celibate clergy. This is an example of how our unconscious can trick and betray us, even our group unconscious, leading us to reluctantly look at realities we would prefer not to face. Properly understood, these betrayals and failures are moments into which redeeming grace may flow. This humbling encounter with forgotten or despised truths of our humanity becomes the threshold to conversion and healed relationships based on compassionate understanding of our commonly-shared weakness.

Oftentimes, well-meaning but misguided religious leaders, parents, and teachers enter the conspiracy by using God as a reinforcement for their efforts to form people according to conventional religious values and social mores which serve to reinforce the development of superficial, public personalities. These superficial personalities, dependent as they are on the approval of society, are the breeding ground of anxieties and neuroses. Our attempts to keep the shadow in its place can, and often does, lead to exaggerated emphasis on external accomplishments, a compulsive and rigid adherence to religious laws and rituals, with a frenetic regimen of activities and enterprises.

Burnout and other forms of spiritual and emotional fatigue are as often as not traceable to unconscious fears of surrendering control of our life. The increasing incidents of burnout and other forms of stress among clergy and religious workers are perhaps more an indication of our fear and avoidance of silence and solitude, with the inevitable encounter with the realities of our life, than it is of too much work.

We find ourselves in a state of double jeopardy. If it is deemed unsafe to reveal aspects of our personality considered "not nice," it is equally hazardous to embrace and creatively live many of our positive, life-giving qualities. Our unredeemed ego is indiscriminate in hiding and repressing not only our evil potential, but our potential for heroism and courage as well. Put another way, when we live according to this subterfuge, our positive potential is repressed and becomes a part of our shadow. Sin and grace become merged. We deny with equal vigor our call to greatness, to virtue. Urges to compassion, to generosity, to heroism and holiness are likewise frowned upon, seen as threats to our established place in a society that puts primary value on self-interest. Thus, when we encounter our "burning bush" or our "annunciation," we manage to avoid dealing with it. Prophetic energy is thwarted, turned inward to sour into angry cynicism or childish, petulant, passive aggression. In place of true prophetic religious practice, we substitute bland and innocuous conventional religiosity. We await the designated hero or heroine sent by "god" to do all the things we think should be done. All the while we seek to avoid the inner voice calling us to be the prophet, the saint we so long for.

Established institutions, whether religious, political or social, put high value on conventional, standardized behavior that reinforces preassigned roles and consensual values. Bold or singular behavior that stretches beyond established standards is considered subversive or an arrogant display of pride. With the willing help of society, parents and teachers, together with religious leaders, energetically suffocate spontaneous creativity in children. In so doing, we encourage them to carve out stilted and calculated personalities, enabling them to fit into cultural stereotypes, preserving and protecting by their docile unquestioning obedience our chosen values. "God" becomes the great rewarder of our efforts and the fierce punisher for our failures. The "god" we worship is no more than the embodiment of our shared cultural delusions.

The end result of this two-way crunch in our psyche is that if we somehow manage to keep the shadow sufficiently under the control of the ego to avoid, at least externally, being revealed as notorious public sinners, we are likewise discouraged from claiming boldly our call to public and courageous prophetic sanctity. Church and society do not encourage us to enter into the adventure of discovering our life's story and authoring its day-to-day telling. Our inner authority is subsumed by external authority, naming the tune to which we are expected to dance. The end result for both church and society is a constituency and membership unable, or unwilling, to think and act independently and creatively, content to accept the shallow comfort of believing that others know better than they about what is good and desirable. Effectively we become the custodians and guardians of our own slavery, presided over by a "god" who gives it divine approbation.

This self-induced hypnotic slumber enables us to uncritically follow our designated political and spiritual leaders and engage in a game of mutual denial of reality. As our ecosystem deteriorates, our social fabric comes apart, morals and ethics disappear not only from our large institutions, but from the neighborhood gas station and appliance repair shop; as our schools become less and less places of learning and the handing on of true values and traditions, as our youth grow more restive, angry and violent, we look every place but to ourselves to find an object to blame or to place our hopes on. We are convinced that it is up to someone else, stronger, more intelligent, more wise and holy to find a solution.

Disenchantment, cynicism, a sense of betrayal overcome the spirit as we realize that even our Church shows an appalling lack of creative imagination, to say nothing of courage, when it comes to providing dynamic leadership on issues that challenge conventional social values. After all, aren't they the product of the same suffocating process, now ordained, and designated to promote and protect the authority of the institution and its place in society? When mediocrity and obsequious, compliant obedience become the political and religious virtues of the day, we reap the rewards of a society without direction, churches marketing superficialities and irrelevant dogma; tinkering and fiddling with liturgical and theological subtleties that please and titillate, in place of the powerful energy of a Gospel call to greatness and world-transforming prophetic energy.

When we persevere in a discipline of attentive, listening prayer, a prayer that attends to the Word of God speaking through our historical circumstances, the resonances of the human anguish within our soul, we begin to probe deeper into the hidden recesses of our inner life. If we can stand the stress of the anxiety and restlessness that comes from silence and personal solitude, we will pierce through to an inner chamber of silence lying beneath our ego defenses. The way through the surface resistance is to be present to it, recognize it and endure it. We will find that beneath the surface turbulence lies a pocket of stillness, a stillness purchased at the cost of enduring resistance from our ego and putting it in its place.

Patient endurance of the discomfort of our silent solitude brings a more stable grounding in the deep of our inner life. Each level of silence is protected by our resistant ego moving deeper and deeper in an effort to find a last stronghold in which to establish its rule. As we move further into our inner life, we will find more forgotten and repressed material waiting to confront us. At each threshold we can either turn and run or face the enemy, silencing it by recognizing it and claiming it as the work of our own hands. Each demon faced and dealt with becomes a threshold point in which we recognize and own our personal participation in the brokenness and sinfulness of humanity. The deeper we go, the more we recognize our common sharing in the lot of humanity and creation. The sins and wickedness previously projected onto others are seen as one's own. The child molester, the rapist, the prostitute, murderer and the like are seen to be mirrors of the common lot of humanity. The distance separating people from one another in the social world of pretense and posturing is diminished as we move to the center of our own self-experience.

In the heart-center we live in conscious union with the divine source of all being; thus union with God in our heart-center is union with all humanity, the saints as well as the sinners, and creation. If sin is our common shared lot, so too is grace. One's eyes are opened to the universal underlying truth shared by all humans, brothers and sisters under God. Namely, that the worst sinner has the potential of being the greatest saint; the greatest saint lives with the possibility of being the greatest sinner. A saint is one who lives in peace with the total truth shared with humanity and creation. A saint is as happy with so-called sinners as with the so-called saints. Both realities are alive and embraced by his or her selfawareness. The sin and the grace within the saint are brought before God in prayer.

Each person lives somewhere on the continuum between personal sinfulness and holiness. Healing grace does not remove us from the taint of sin, but makes us aware of the fact that even in our worst sin, our most abject failure, we are infinitely loved, the object of divine compassion; even at the heights of our graced moments, we are totally dependent on Divine Mercy, for even at that graced moment we continue to share in the sinful condition of others.

Prayer is not so much our personal program of making ourselves pleasing to God, separating us from the "sinners," but rather a surrender into the God-life within, the same potential for grace that we share with all humanity. As this prayer deepens and reawakens us to the truth of our self, our sense of who we are and what we are called to be opens us to the grace that is already ours, waiting to flood into our lives and release the God-like qualities that have heretofore been suffocated by our self-imposed darkness. In this process, God's life and human life are joined. We become our prayer. Our lives are touched and enlivened by the infinite and eternal, our deep soul is now nourished, strengthened and anointed by our living awareness of the eternal kingdom present now, even as we experience the reality of our unfinished journey into fullness. "In the abundance of his glory may he, through his Spirit, enable you to grow firm in power with regard to your inner self, so that Christ may live in your hearts through faith, and then, planted in love and built on love, with all God's holy people you will have the strength to grasp the breadth and the length, the height and the depth; so that, knowing the love of Christ, which is beyond knowledge, *you may be filled with the utter fullness of God*" (Eph. 3:16-19 NJB). Such is the awesome reality that we allow into our lives at that moment in which we open our minds and hearts to the living God in the act we have come to call prayer.

Conclusion

I have attempted to present biblical images that reveal the fundamental model of the nature of our relationship to God. It has been my objective to show that our tradition is one of ennobling and empowering the person by revealing the sacred quality of our time-earthbound condition. Revelation challenges us to establish and maintain proper, harmonious relationships in which human consciousness enlarges beyond the boundaries of egocentric perceptions to include persons, animals, plants, the very heart of the earth herself. I propose that God cannot be truly known, served and worshipped without this fundamental acceptance of the biblical revelation of the sacred, life-giving relationship with all dimensions of creation.

We are not blind, passive victims of impersonal forces, but creators, artists forging a reign of peace and justice in which Divine Wisdom rules the affairs of men and women. Our biblical heroes and heroines are models of people who discover and exercise creative power over the events of their lives and the forces of history. I hoped to show that an encounter with God is a creative and dynamic event that shifts and enlarges the center of one's awareness to include all of history and every aspect of creation. This results in new relationships through the emergence of a sense of responsibility for oneself and the quality of one's participation in life. We live and act from a realization that all things exist and have their being in the One God. The human person becomes the sacrament of redemptive action modeled by Jesus the Christ, the New Adam: the true you, the true me. This is the freedom of the Gospel, the marriage of our spirit with the Holy Spirit of God. "Don't you know that you yourselves are God's temple and that God's Spirit lives in you?" (1 Cor. 3:16 NJB).

Prayer and spirituality are the ground of our disciplined and focused efforts to find the lost truth of our hidden self and to allow that true self the freedom to grow into its ordained union with the Divine.

Prayer and creative spiritual expression are innate to the human person; they preexist public religious expression and creed-based church membership. It is not uncommon to find life-giving spirituality and a genuine life of prayer existing without the aid of organized religion or of church affiliation.

Spirituality, an innate quality of the human person, is the ground out of which public, organized religious structures must grow. Authentic prayer and spiritual expression provide the energy to creatively write the story of our life. Through spiritual understanding our life becomes our poem, our song and our gift to creation. Life is discovered, expressed and given in humble service. The role of religion and church is to help in discovering the poetic spiritual expession of one's unique life.

Religion, church, and spirituality are not interchangeable terms. Spirituality is the preexistent ground out of which our insertion into life is established. It is the primal stuff out of which our unique personality is formed and from which we seek meaningful relationships. Depending on the quality of this primal experience, our efforts at relationships, our skills in coping with the challenges of life are determined. To be out of touch with this primary, personal experience of one's participation in life, and then to expect that religion or church membership will have significance, is futile. Our participation in religion and church membership is at best determined by the quality of our primary, prereligious experiences. When church is alive and creative with prophetic leadership complemented by a mature membership, it can become the means whereby one is awakened to recognize a personal need for spiritual nourishment. With the aid of authentic religious experience, our spiritual hungers are addressed, given direction.

Religion is the social, consensual expression of humanity's united and commonly-shared struggle to make life make sense, to give it order and direction towards a goal. Religion helps us enter into the mysterious imponderables of life by offering the hope of finding life-giving significance, by connecting us with others through shared symbols and stories. Authentic religious expression, with its myths and public rituals, provides form and focus to express and share the poetry of our individual spiritual expression. If religion needs to be open to receive and guide our innate spiritual quest, we need a corresponding open and vital connection to our personal spiritual hunger.

Church, with its dogmas, creeds and laws, is a more specific way of being religious, a more immediate way of gathering the religious quest into definable limits and pointing it in a specific direction. Church gathers us into a community with articulated dogmas and creeds aiding in the process through which we understand and give expression to our unique participation in history. Church provides a specific public identity enabling a community to gather and celebrate in ritual a sense of shared purpose and self-understanding. When Church works, it provides the ground from which one is free to be open and in dialogue with the world, to harmonize one's particular spiritual quest with others, to contribute as well as receive the shared wisdom of other traditions. Our role in the process is to bring to the experience of church a vital and active prayer life, enabling the mysteries celebrated to penetrate and address our solitary spiritual search.

Religion and church find their most authentic expression by being joined together in the task of serving the spiritual quest for authentic living. That quest is experienced by individual persons in specific places, under specific circumstances, in a given time in history. Each person is called to be energetically engaged in the task of discovering the meaning of one's life. This responsibility cannot be abdicated to others, nor can its expression be adapted to conform to the expectations of others. Religion and church establish their valid authority by being communities in which persons experience the freedom and support from others, from tradition, and from the wisdom of the leaders to boldly live their mystery.

In and of themselves religion and church have no inherent value. Without being rooted in real human issues, they fall into a series of magic, superstitious beliefs and practices that delude and narcotize the human spirit. Instead of being a means to an end, they become their own reason for being, all efforts being directed toward the perpetuation of their own structures and authority. Rather than being servants of the Word addressing the deep spiritual hungers of persons, persons become the spiritual slaves to church structures with their laws and fossilized traditions.

The Word of God is addressed to persons struggling within the confusing and bewildering turmoil of life. Beneath all church structures and religious practices there remains in our tradition a living, historical person who claimed to be the "Way, the Truth and the Life" (Jn.14:6). Unless religion and church mediate a personal encounter between individual persons, each in their unique time and place, with this living historical person, Jesus, the religious enterprise becomes a stumbling block to its own avowed purposes. When Jesus is allowed to mediate the Christ-event in individual lives, conversion and empowerment happen. The Christ-event takes flesh in our time and place. The person's spiritual quest is enlarged to become one, through Christ, with all people of all times, as well as with the unfolding of creation.

Religion and church together are the midwife and womb, respectively, within which authentic life is generated, birthed and formed into truly free and self-possessed, contemplative, mystic prophets. True religion can be an awesome force for the creation of a people bonded together in a common vision of the truly noble and sacred nature of humanity and creation. "For the Kingdom of God is not a matter of talk but of power" (1 Cor. 4:20 NJB).

Christians profess to be a Resurrection-Pentecost people called by the Spirit and sent to proclaim the Good News to all creation. ". . . you will receive the power of the Holy Spirit which will come on you, and then you will be my witnesses not only in Jerusalem but throughout Judea and Samaria, and indeed to earth's remotest end" (Acts 1:8 NJB). Pentecost is described as a great wind accompanied by tongues of fire as the disciples experienced the power of the Holy Spirit come upon them (Acts 2:1-4).

The point I want to emphasize is that we believe ourselves to be a people who have an immediate claim on God's Holy Spirit living and acting in history through individual human lives lived in union with that Spirit (1 Cor. 2:10-12). God has claimed Divine authority over the hearts of all men and women, without the interference or manipulation of arbitrary human authority. The church is called to be the mother in whose womb this audacious freedom is nourished. Like a mother, church must recognize that she does not have final, absolute authority over the life within her, but is the guardian and teacher guiding and directing that life towards its destined maturity. In maturity one is able to live autonomously, while remaining responsible and accountable to the larger community.

The Holy Spirit has been poured out upon the community of believers and not just ordained men. The fundamental relationship between church leadership and people, who are the church, is one of trusting, mature dialogue. When the community of faith is segmented into authoritative structures of coercive power, the dialogue of trust and mutual reverence is violated.

For human beings, individually or corporately, to usurp the authority of God and interpret it in defense of their own authority and the preservation of their power is an outrageous infringement into Divine prerogatives. If church authority so fears heresy and creative personal freedom that she suffocates the free initiative of God's Spirit living in and inspiring the faithful, she sins against the free initiative of the Word and Spirit she is called to serve.

Likewise, for individuals to denigrate and despise their personal role and responsibility in bringing about the work of the Spirit in their lives is, I believe, an offense against the reign of the Spirit. This we do when we abdicate our personal authority for life and action in favor of external authority upon whom we project our need for surrogate parents.

We believe that the overall divine plan is to bring about the reign of God on earth as it is in heaven. Jesus taught us to pray to the Father: ". . . may your Kingdom come, your will be done on earth as it is in heaven . . ." Human beings united to Divine Wisdom through the Holy Spirit are the instruments of this plan and the church is the mother and teacher. Healthy and loving mothers and teachers nourish life and welcome the transition from dependency to responsible and enlightened freedom as a testimony to the success of their efforts.

Individually and in community we are a people gathered together in faith. Together we listen, discern and respond to God's Word and become the contemplative, mystical and prophetic people in the tradition of Moses, Mary, Christ, and the apostles and saints right down to our own time. It is their modern day counterparts that we most need today. *"If today you hear God's voice . . ."*